CELEBRATE
LIFE'S LESSONS

Marene J. Austin

BALBOA.
PRESS

A DIVISION OF HAY HOUSE

Marene J. Austin's editors were: Jeanne Brandon & Curzetta Monique' Austin.

Author Credits: AAS Degree, Radiologic Technology, Founder CEO, Entrepreneur, Jewelry Artist, Motivational Speaker, Life Emprovement Coach.

Scripture taken from the King James Version of the Bible.

Balboa Press books may be ordered through booksellers or by contacting:

Balboa Press
A Division of Hay House
1663 Liberty Drive
Bloomington, IN 47403
www.balboapress.com
1-(877) 407-4847

Printed in the United States of America.

ISBN: 978-1-4525-7561-2 (sc)
ISBN: 978-1-4525-7560-5 (e)

Balboa Press rev. date: 06/12/2013

To All My "Ride or Die" Family & friends

Traci Abram, Curzetta Austin, Kathleen Marx-Bancoft,
Allie & Renae Bond,
Patricia Cagle, Viola Coleman,
Rita Hayes, Charity Hicks, Dorothy & Lowell Hicks,
Danny Illoube, Sherri & Michael Jeffries,
Mary Johnson, Nathaniel & Renee Jones, Odessa Jones,
Myrtle Luss, Dorothy Mason, Andrea Hicks-
Mathews, Louise Miller, Marjorie Moore,
LaVita Lewis, Dana Lynn, Debra & Jim Moore,
Freda Mukes, Ronald Nelson,
Fred & Bernise Newsom, Richard Presberry, Marie Smith, Natacha
Smith, Janice Twillie, Martha Watkins and Nathifa Young.

All of you all pushed me off my cliff while I was doing this
book project and throughout my life! You made sure I
didn't quit or give up on anything that I set out to do.
You pushed me, shoved, kicked, slapped and loved me into shape!
You believed in me and always told me that I could depend on
your listening ears and your prayers of support. Sometimes
I ranted, raved, whined and other times I simply motivated
and preached, yet you remained my audience. Your quiet and
sometimes rumpus support continually sustains me.
You were and will always be my watchful angels!

A Special Thanks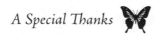

A Special Tribute!

To my life-long love, Curtis B. Austin, you loved me until death did us part. Thanks! I miss your patient, humble presence. Love Mae!

To Chegieta Chantele' Austin-Drinkard. My dear second child, you left me far too soon. I miss you and I will always love you! Mama.

To Aretha Bradley, my long gone bestest best friend. Your support left a high wind under my wings!

To Bernice Stone, my late sister-in-law, you rescued me when I needed a place to stay. Thanks!

A special thanks to all my fun & faithful five daughters: Lavita Fonnette Lewis, Chegieta Chantele' Austin-Drinkard, (In heaven) Roshun Antoinette Austin, Curzetta Monik' Austin & Charity Matrissa Austin-Hicks

And to all my grand children: Destiny Garrett, Tamar Austin, Jari Head, Everette Spears, Kyla Lewis, Kieva Lewis, Abeni Hicks, Lailah Wilson, Nicole Hicks, Erica Hicks, Joy Hicks and Grace Hicks.

Table of Contents

Chapter 1

I Had a Dream

I had a dream. I dreamed that the world had changed. Everything was different and nothing was still the same. CHANGE HAD BEEN FORCED UPON US! My dream lasted three night times. It seemed like that for a while, every single time that I went to bed and fell asleep, I started dreaming, something.

The first night, I dreamed that there were lots of women lying out on the ground in an open field screaming, crying and bleeding. All of them were in pain. Something had happened to them and apparently they had been given up on by the mainstream sources in society that had the capacity to help them. There I was, in the middle of nowhere all by myself without any resources to help those women. All I had was a great big heart! Anyway, I was willing to help them in any way that I could because all of them were hurting, bleeding and damaged in some way. The fact that they were bleeding made me feel a strong compassion to want to help them. But, what could I actually do that would bring some relief to those women?

There was one thing that I knew for sure, and that was that I needed to do something. So, I just started running around in circles, trying to help everybody. I was moving through that stream of women, running from woman to woman. I stepped over some of them and I jumped over some of the others trying to work on all of them at one time. I knew that if

1

I used my common sense, I could help a little. I was tying tourniquets to stop the bleeding, rubbing pain spots, offering encouraging words, crying with some and inspiring others. That process became somewhat slow because there were far too many people out there than one person could humanly serve.

Then, I started feeling overwhelmed at the brokenness that I was witnessing! My compassion was at its highest peak and all those women could feel it out there in that open field. They felt it even in places that I couldn't possibly physically touch. It seemed like all the women had so many issues. They appeared to be hurting over various situations in life and I felt compelled to try to stop the bleeding. I got so involved in the process of stopping the bleeding and easing their pain that I became extremely tired and sweaty, as I tried to help everybody. Then, when I woke up the next morning, I could still hear women voices in the back of my mind, crying in that open field. They were all moaning, groaning, shouting and screaming, "H E L P!" When I got out of the bed, I said to myself, "Hmm!" "What was that all about? That was a whole "Field of Pain!" Is God trying to tell me something?"

The next night after I went to bed and fell asleep, I started dreaming again. That time my dream was about the church.

At that time in my life I very entrenched in church work. It seemed like church was the totality of my social life. I was raised in a church conscience environment and I thought that I had to go to church every time the church door opened. My parents made church a key part of everything we did back in the day. Therefore, I was carrying out the same type upbringing with my own children of which I was very accustomed. Going to church it seemed, was a regular routine part of my life, like breathing is a regular function of my respiratory system. That routine had served me very well though, in terms of discipline and moral principles. I was always very involved in church work and I was so faithful to the church that sometimes I let my life go and sometimes I even let my family go. We had to go to church now and deal with life later. The trouble was that it seemed like we never really took the time to deal with life. My husband and I combined our efforts. We allowed others to project their opinions of what was right for us and for our family. We pretty much walked around in denial most of the time in our young lives adopting the concept that, "God will fix this and God will fix that." We didn't have a clue that we had to participate and fix some things for ourselves if we had the ability to fix them.

Sometimes it appeared as if we felt compelled to spend most of our time in life trying to live up to everybody else's expectations. At that time in my life I was more focused on how other people saw me. I wanted them to see me as the "perfect Christian," and my desire was to live up to their version of the "perfect Christian." The trouble was that there were so many variations of the "perfect Christian," that I was having a hard time measuring up. I really wanted to be accepted by those church folks. But somehow, I later realized that my focus, drive and my inner God's given talents had been lost in that maze.

Anyway, the second night, I dreamed that the church had been exposed. The real church was being revealed and it didn't look so hot after all. Some of those preachers who had always been looked up to and reverenced by the masses had been exposed. Some of the things that had been done in the dark had started to come to the light and, it seemed like those preachers were walking around on their heads.

In that dream some of the church people had started saying that they were embarrassed to even be associated with preachers and the church. I was bewildered over all of that! It seemed like so many preachers had failed God that the preachers' ratings had started to drop to an all time low. There seemed to be an exchange in power. It seemed as though more women were becoming involved in the leadership of ministry to make up for the failures that had been created by some of those false leaders. At the end of that dream, a voice spoke to me and said that I would be **"Running a Revival but it would not be held in the church. This revival would be in the streets."** When I got up the next day I said to myself; "A REVIVAL IN THE STREETS?" Oh No! No, not me! I can't do stuff like that, I thought. People will start thinking that I am insane! Then, I thought to myself, what is really going on here?

Again, when I went to bed on the third night, I dreamed that I was running! I was running very fast behind a Black Stallion. I was actually keeping up with that darn horse. He was running in the light of the day and he was running in the dark of the night and I was simply keeping up with him. I was running right behind that Black Stallion and I was doing whatever I saw that horse do. If the horse ran, I ran. If the horse walked, I walked. If the horse trotted, I trotted. If he jumped a wide ditch of water, I jumped over a wide ditch of water. If the horse slowed down and walked again, I slowed down and walked. Then, suddenly it seemed like out of nowhere, a voice shouted out to me, **"RUN WITH THE VISION! RUN WITH THE VISION! RUN WITH THE VISION!"** I could hear that voice all night in my sleep. Finally, I got with the rhythm of that voice and I started chanting along with the voice while I ran behind the Black Stallion. **"RUN WITH THE VISION, RUN WITH THE VISION, RUN WITH THE VISION,"** I kept up with that horse while running at the same pace. Then, I looked down and noticed that I had a "Scroll" in my hand and I also noticed that I was tightly gripping that Scroll. This must be the Vision, I thought, and it must be written on this Scroll. And I was holding on to it as tightly as I could while running behind the Black Stallion.

All night long I was running right behind that Black Stallion in my dream. Sometimes the horse and I ran so long and hard that it often seemed like we were floating. Then there were times when we would slow down to the slowest pace and rest a little. I just kept my eyes on the horse as I continued to do whatever the horse did while I held on to the Vision which was written on that Scroll. There were times when we were only trotting and still that voice was saying slowly; "Run with the Vision," "Run with the Vision," Run with the Vision." Then suddenly, it seemed like, right out of the middle of nowhere in the dark of the night, something would happen again and the horse would take off! It was like suddenly a shock or something would trigger that horse and cause him to take off. Then, that voice would pick up it's pace, and there we were, running again. The voice was crying out again, **"RUN WITH THE VISION, RUN WITH THE VISION, RUN WITH THE VISION!** There I was again keeping up with the horse. Then, I started chanting along with the voice, **"RUN WITH THE VISION, RUN WITH THE VISION, RUN WITH THE VISION,"** until my husband finally shook me, woke me up and said, "Girl what in the world is wrong with you? I think you may need to see a doctor or something, Marene. Maybe your blood pressure is up. You are just hollering and making loud noises in your sleep. WHAT IN THE WORLD IS WRONG WITH YOU! You need to get a hold of yourself girl," "Lawd have mercy!"

I woke up the next morning in a daze! I still could hear that voice in the back of my mind and in my spirit I was still chanting, **"RUN WITH THE VISION, RUN WITH THE VISION, RUN WITH THE VISION,"** and that black horse, what was the meaning of all that stuff? And, those dreams! JESUS, Am I losing it? I was very perplexed! Those dreams had really started to get my attention which caused me to stop and think. Maybe this is an OMEN, I thought! I had just experienced three consecutive nights of dreams. I could actually envision that there must be some type of significant meaning to those dreams. OH, MY GOD! What is going on here, I thought to myself. It never occurred to me at that time, while following that experience of dreams, that my life would turn around and go in a different direction. This would ultimately cause me to change forever. Although, it did occur to me that those dreams could possibly represent something spiritual.

After having those dreams, I started siphoning something significant from almost everything that happened to me. My life was actually never again going to be the same. A major transformation had taken place, but at that time, I couldn't really describe what it was. It started feeling like a special calling had been placed upon my life. However, I started thinking to myself; "calling to do what, and how?" I couldn't imagine what was really going on at that time. I really didn't know what to do, but I did know that I certainly would be doing something. I couldn't stop thinking about those dreams. It seemed like every time I found myself alone, I would start thinking about those dreams again. I was always trying to drum up my own interpretation and I was getting nowhere fast. I knew for sure that I had experienced something real and very unusual in my life.

I started taking a different look at my own life. I was moved to recognize and research for ways to find my own purpose for being born. I decided to concentrate on what was most important in my life. I became very focused on almost everything that I did after those dreams because I had lots of things on my mind. I already knew that I had lots of talents to offer to this society and I wanted to learn how to make my life count for something. I also knew that I could use my talents right where I was in life. I recognized that I was beautifully and wonderfully made and I knew that I had been created for greatness! Thoughts constantly fired in my spiritual psyche and caused me to revisit my own personal value system.

I decided that I would stop accepting the status quo. The first thing I had to do was to start using my own brain and thinking more for myself and making more independent decisions in my life. I knew that I had a right to draw my own conclusions from what I was thinking. Sometimes, I asked myself several questions like what were I going to do with myself now that God had shown me those dreams? How can I move myself into the right direction for my life? I knew that I had a purpose because my mama used to always tell me that she could see something in me, even when I was a very young girl. I often found myself sitting alone day dreaming. There were times when I brought up that picture of myself running with a vision in that dream. I was inquisitive as to how I would be able to find that vision and learn how to get on with it in my life. I also wanted to know what that Black Stallion meant and how I could figure out how to put that information together and make it work for me.

Surely, there must be a destiny for me and I am going to find it, I thought. I was desperate to discover why I was born. I knew that everybody had been beautifully and wonderfully made in their right season for a specific reason. I also knew that when the time was right that I would be willing to step into my place on the platform of life and play my part. God had plugged a component in me that would engage the talent that came packaged inside me at birth.

My authenticity separated me from everyone else. Nobody could be **Marene** except **Marene** because I was stamped with a "Seal of Authenticity" at birth and that could not be duplicated. I knew that God had placed a specific spiritual assignment on my life. I also knew that I had to fulfill that assignment in the universe because nobody else could fulfill my assignment accept me. Additionally, I knew that what had happened to me in those three nights of dreams was no coincidence. The time had come for me to use my life's experiences and lessons to paint a picture of my works to leave for the next generation. Some of the things that I had learned in life could and would become valuable lessons from which others could and would learn. I had so much to look forward to and I was very excited about all of this awakening!

Satisfaction and complacency were no longer acceptable positions in my life. I had a thirst and I was searching for something, but what was it? When I experienced certain incidents in my life, I started looking at them as life lessons. I started asking myself, "What can I learn from that good or bad experience?" **We can always learn lessons after the tears, disappointments, disasters and setbacks in life. Then we can say that this experience can and will only make me better. Marene, 101.**

A great spiritual assignment had been placed on my life. I had been assigned to do something positive in the wake of my experiences. I adopted a faith mind-set and would never let go! I learned how to believe that when something happened in my life that could or would possibly devastate me; I learned to listen to my inner voice and allow it to drive me towards my destiny. I never knew what to expect but I did know that I was finding direction for my life.

Suddenly, I felt pregnant again, however, this time it was a spiritual pregnancy. A special seed had been planted inside my spiritual fallopian tubes and it had been ovulated. Something great was growing inside my womb and someday I would give birth to that new baby. It had to be the "gift" that was being groomed in my womb and society would have to make room to receive what I had to offer. I was going to leave a legacy for the next generation. My own talents were starting to surface and they were bubbling inside me. I was on to something here! I would literally sometimes shake all over with excitement as I envisioned creating ideas and innovations that were being manufactured inside my own mind.

After those dreams I often felt motivated and excited because I was feeling exhilaration in the air which was causing me to start working quietly and alone to develop my visions and dreams. I left no room for interference keeping all of this to myself while sorting things out. Nobody else was involved so my thoughts would not be influenced.

I started recognizing incidents as they happened in my life and viewed them as life lessons. Then I chose to become a good student of life. Consequently, it became much easier for me to deal with difficult circumstances in my life because I could always subtract the victim mentality and sum up the purpose for the experience. As it is stated, the truth hurts, so people have a tendency to blame someone or something else when they are ultimately responsible for what happens to them in their own lives. **Victim mentality often lurks around to evade the minds of people who experience uncontrollable misfortunes in life. Marene, 101.** I made happiness my choice because happiness for me was not based on the circumstances that often occurred in my life. I learned to accept the concept that things could always be worse and that I was better off than some people.

People often stated that they enjoyed being associated with me and some even expressed that they were inspired after talking with me, or listening to me talk. I had the propensity to look at the bright side of everything. Even if I did cry over certain situations, I eventually found the meaning of and the purpose for the experience. Sometimes I would ask myself, what is life trying to teach me from this experience and what will I take away from this? I enjoyed turning the negative into the positive. Being positive became a sport for me. It seemed like when situations in my life seemed to stagger me, a spirit of motivation would overtake me. The sport activity came when I could end up winning over certain situations with a positive attitude. That attitude always made me feel much better about different situations.

I found it intriguing to become a renegade and look at things from a different perspective than other people seemed to see them. I would create my own perspective. When people would sum up situations and judge them as hopeless, I would look at the same situations from my own positive angle and seek for the lessons to be learned.

I also learned how to listen to other people's views and respect their opinions. **Another way to experience pain in life is to try changing other people. Marene, 101.** Respect for people helped me to listen to their views and then procure my own viewpoint. I had my own opinion and I had a right to draw my own conclusions. I committed to embracing my choices on matters in my life. There are some things that we just owe ourselves. I had a right to operate in my own individuality. I am Marene and there is only one Marene in the whole wide world.

A spirit of passion was bestowed upon me for everything I did! That passion derived mainly from learning how to process my own life based on whatever I believed in. Then I started feeling an atmosphere of freedom! I would no longer lend my mind to others and be swayed by their opinions unless I wanted to. I had gained my own freedom of thoughts!

Chapter 2

Mama-Nem

The three nights of dreams continued to weigh in the back of my mind even when I was preoccupied doing other things. I often felt like something spiritual was going on inside my mind. I remembered back when I was a child how my parents raised me C.O.G.I.C. I grew up during a time when they said that there was a Pentecostal Movement. Mama-nem used to say things like; "One for the Father," One for the Son," And, One for the Holy Ghost." That statement was often chanted while we were at church. I started thinking to myself Hmm, three nights of dreams . . . maybe that was something much bigger than me! It was in fact, bigger than life! I knew that I was on to something, but what was it? I kept processing through those thoughts on a daily basis.

As I again reflected on my childhood, it seemed like back then, that everything those grown ups did at church, they spiritualized. They would get happy, dance and prophecy. Some of them even predicted peoples' marriages, death, and some of the other important events that would happen in individuals' lives. As a child I was very scared of prophecy because I feared death. Those prophecy sessions used to make me feel like we were having a séance or something. They made loud and sad public moans and cries in the church. They often interrupted the order of worship with speaking in tongues and prophesying. Since I was the self made musician for the church, I was mandated by my mama to attend every service.

During those prophecies, other parishioners would sit there and quietly pray and cry. I was simply a terrified little girl! They were always "seeing" things. Lawd, I was so afraid of that activity. Then sometimes after church services, they would sit around and talk about their night dreams and visions. It seemed like that was our entertainment back then. People barely had televisions in their households back in the day. There were only a few televisions sets in the whole neighborhood. Thus, when we went to church it was our entertainment.

We were also allowed to go to the movies and while we were at the movies we knew we'd better remember to separate ourselves in that colored section that divided us from the white people. We also had a favorite jump spot up town. My parents did not allow us to participate in what they considered the devil's dens back when I was a child. Since I was Pentecostal I had to sneak and party because they always called us sinners and carnal when we tried to have fun. I also grew up back in the sixties during the Civil Rights Movement.

Caruthersville, MO where I grew up was a sleepy little town located in the bottom of the county and it was called the "Bootheel" in Pemiscot County. We had a very small population of around 6,700 people. When I was a child, most families' income derived from picking and chopping cotton. While we did have a few educators such as teachers, most of the community was made up of common people and hand laborers. Most residents worked in the cotton patches or soy bean fields. The socio-economic status was made up mostly of poor people in my neighborhood. Although the word poor were never mentioned, the average family survived from picking and chopping cotton. I don't recall ever hearing statements like, average income status. Your average income derived from how much cotton you had a chance to chop or pick if the weather permitted you to work. We all worked very hard in those cotton patches. Additionally, my parents also worked on other domestic jobs to provide for our family.

Obviously, we had a few school teachers, a principal, a janitor, a doctor and a school bus driver. They were considered the high class people in our community back in the day. Everybody else was field hands.

My parents were good citizens who focused on living right and working hard to raise and educate their children. They taught us the golden rule which was, "treat other people the way you want them to treat you." We shared a loving and supportive family unit. We were taught to stick together, love one another, look out for one another, and by all means, keep our business to yourself.

Since my parents were very religious my mama made it a point to expose me to various types of religious denominations. That served as a plus in helping me to maintain an open mind. As I reminisce, there were as many hang ups as there were religious differences. It seemed like every denomination believed that they had the keys to heavens doors. All of that talk and the debates over who was right and who was saved kept me thoroughly confused. I learned how to mind my own business and keep my opinion to myself. But even then, I had a right to my own opinion. I didn't know the difference as a child, so I believed whatever my parents believed. I became accustomed to praying before meals, and sometimes we had to fast and pray so we could be blessed.

Things were very sparse back then and we had to almost live off the land. We raised gardens in the summer and canned food for the winter and believe me, everybody in the family who were big enough, had to help with all of the work. Then, when the food ran out in the winter we learned how to pick wild greens off the levy to make our meals. I believe those wild greens would translate to dandelions in today's world. That was all about our survival. My tenacity was developed from learning how to improvise back in the day.

My mama and daddy were go getters and taught all their children how to go out there and get 'em! There were also times during the winter months when it seemed like there was nothing for us to eat. During those times mama-nem threw bread crumbs out on the ground to attract birds. Next, mama rigged up an old headboard of a bed, tied a long cord to the headboard and then she propped it up with a big stick. The bread crumbs attracted birds under the headboard and once a large number of birds were feasting on the bread crumbs, mama then jerked the cord that was drawn through the kitchen window and she killed a ton of birds for dinner that day. I can still picture those images in my mind's eye. We could see a thousand little bird legs sticking up in the air on the kitchen table. As children we were taught to make things happen instead of making excuses.

Mama also used to tell us stories about her spiritual dreams that she had while she was sleeping at night. That left an indelible impression on my mind. She often explained how God gave her directions and visions for her future. She was kind and loving, yet very firm. She was a hard working woman and she was always cooking and singing, it seemed. I want to emphasize the singing! We could always get away with our devilment because the loud singing was our signal that mama was in the area. Both of my parents worked together and instilled in their children that we could be the best at everything that we did. They set a good example for us to follow. They were strict about us keeping our business to ourselves and they were not playing either. Both mama and daddy possessed good work ethic. They taught us with their lives. I always admired my mama's determination because she was fearless, courageous and resilient.

Mama lived on the straight and narrow and she was always trying to please God with her life. It seemed like I couldn't figure out what God wanted because it seemed like he was asking for so much. It seemed like almost everything we did was wrong so I made sure that I got saved every Sunday.

Mama surely had premonition! She would literally predict peoples' life events and even their death. She seemed to know when someone was carrying a gun and all kinds of stuff. She also often predicted storms and other important incidents. She simply had a special gift in that area. Both of my parents were always summing things up with some kind of purpose and destination. You can imagine how my upbringing somewhat influenced my spiritual mind-set. I was a serious little girl and I was always thinking, probably too much at times. What was God doing up there?

In addition to all of that spiritual activity, my Aunt Lillie who raised my mama, was always calling me a little sinner because I would get happy and dance on the floor at church with the grown-ups. She was always at church looking for, waiting on and watching out for me. And, when she caught me dancing she used to sneak up behind me and pop me on the behind for playing with God! That used to be very funny to the other children who saw her do that to me and it embarrassed me! Anyway, I was determined to dance at church. I learned and did that dance with the grown-ups. I loved dancing at church!

Chapter 3

Those Dreams Surfaced Again

After I experienced those three nights of dreams, I noticed that something new, exciting and different was happening in my life. It was like I was coming into my Bar Mitzvah or something. In my opinion things like having those three nights of dreams didn't randomly happen to someone. Maybe I am special after all, I thought. I actually could have been born to serve a special purpose on this earth. I felt that maybe there was a true anointing on my life like some of the other people on this planet. I started digging a little deeper inside myself and analyzing my life from another angle. I could be actually finding my calling in life here, and if so, I was going to also leave some footprints in the sand. WOW! That was all about me and nobody else. The puzzle pieces of my life were being laid in the right places. My life was shaping into a beautiful picture. That type of thinking was causing me to become lightheaded with excitement! That was mostly because my vocation was shaping up and the outcome was going to be positive!

I literally formed a personal "think tank" and started programming questions in my mind like; how can I find the steps that I needed to take to get this special work done? I also made it a point not to allow obstacles to hinder me or to stop me from thinking positively about my life. Nothing or nobody was going to hinder or deter me from finding my answers. I was headed somewhere and it was thrilling. It felt exciting to feel the pulse beat of my destination inside my spirit. I was moving in the right direction in my life. At the end of each day I thought about my accomplishments for that day. Everything I did played a major role in helping me to understand, discover and fulfill my God given purpose.

The next thing I decided to do was to keep track of my daily progress whether I was at work or at home. It didn't matter what I was charting, I wanted to see progress. Calculating my accomplishments felt like I was saving money or something of great value. I was storing accomplishments in my memory bank and using them to propel me along the way. That was like a new bank account. At the end of every month I could look back and calculate how many accomplishments I had developed on my personal balance sheet.

I never allowed myself to stop thinking that way. Processing my life's dream became a regular part of my body's functions like breathing. I was breeding something new and different! Good and positive thoughts consistently evaded my mind and I was enjoying all this! I had a private positive process going on inside my mind which was causing me to create new ideas. I had a little valuable "nugget" inside me and nobody would ever take it away from me.

A person can formulate ideas and become as creative as she wants to. Marene, 101. As time passed, I felt a little overwhelmed because it seemed like things weren't coming together fast enough for me. Oh, how I wanted my ten thousand pieces "life puzzle" to manifest something for me overnight, but I had to learn that various events in life created the 10,000 piece life puzzle. Oh God, this is going to take a while.

I started to rebel against my own thoughts. How was I going to carry out a calling when I didn't even know what it was? I guess I was looking for a lighting bolt experience. Later, I had to accept the fact that, **"life just happens and experiences in life, good, bad or indifferent, are designed to teach lessons." Marene, 101.** Ultimately, I had to adapt to changes as they took place in my life. That thought taught me how to slow myself down occasionally and process the courses of my life in small steps.

I am not a victim. I am a seed that has been planted in this society to grow something great! I was called for purpose; purpose was not called for me. Marene, 101.

Let me see, I thought. Those women that I dreamed about that were lying out on the ground in that open "Field of Pain" apparently needed something that I had. I was running with a "Scroll" in my hand and a voice was saying, "Run with the Vision." I had been given the awesome task of helping the ladies. They were out there waiting on me to fulfill my assignment so they could stop the hurting. And the Scroll, was that the vision that I was holding in my hand?' Hmm, "maybe this is my anointing?" I thought out loud. I also noticed that often things worked out for me as if I had a certain favor over my life or something. I had to continually remember that I didn't go out there looking for that "Scroll." I looked down at my hand and recognized that it (the Scroll) was in my hand and I was holding on to it very tightly. After recognizing the scroll in that dream, a voice had spoken to me and told me to **"Run With the Vision."** Hmm, I thought, that must be my product, "Those hurting women." So I would start at that point figuring out how I would work with the concept that I was starting to gather from my dreams.

First, I had to learn how to learn. Then I had to learn the lessons that life were teaching me. Next, I had to learn how to allow those lessons to benefit me so I could become pliable and strong. Then, I would be able to help others from my own experiences and my own life's story. There was no room for me to allow life to devastate me. The experiences that I was encountering were going to become teachable lessons. If I learned how to manage my own pain and sort it in the right places in my life then I could in turn, teach other women how to manage their pain. Then we could all "Celebrate Life's Lessons" together! That outlook helped me to develop a strong coping mechanism as life brought obstacles my way.

Chapter 4

Here Goes the "For Better or For Worse" Tests

The first devastating thing that happened to me when I was a very young lady was that my husband was seriously burned using gasoline to light the barbeque grill. There wasn't anyone else outside with him that day. He told me that after he walked away from the grill it felt as if something was crawling up his leg. Then when he looked down, there was a trail of fire that had followed him and one of his pants legs was on fire. He said that he then fell down and started rolling on the ground in an effort to put the fire out. He also thought that he accidentally swallowed some flames. Ultimately, he suffered second and third degree burns over a large portion of his body and he was hospitalized close to two weeks.

Again, about a year later while working at his carpenter' job where he was building a room for a co-worker, while using a skills saw, he accidentally sawed his right arm wide open and severed one of his fingers causing severe muscle and ligament damage. They rushed him to the hospital and the doctor said that he would need emergency surgery. The doctors predicted that he would never work again especially because he was a carpenter and since there was major damage to his right arm and hand. However, the first miracle was that the surgeon was able to save his arm.

Needless to say, he defied the odds and a few months later, he was able to return to his carpenter job and use that damaged arm again.

Then, a couple years later, Curtis started feeling weak and had shortness of breath for a few weeks before he finally gave in and saw a doctor. After a series of testing and hospital stays we learned that he had been stricken with a debilitating muscle disease called "Polymyositis." That was a rare muscle disease and at that time we were told that Medical Science did not know very much about it. They recorded some of their findings from Curtis's treatments on his disease in the Medical Journal. We were also told that some researches revealed that in the past, some people had lived only about six months after being diagnosed.

I felt devastated at the onset of that disappointing news. Then I thought that I must look up to my only Source for strength. All our family, close friends and church members were concerned and supportive. However, I was the person who had to choose to focus on the faith that I had heard so much about, but barely had had such an opportunity to exercise it. As I started to deal with this life inflicting reality I thought to myself, God must be teaching me something here again. It was strange how so many unexpected things were beginning to happen in our lives. We were greeted with adversity without a clue as to what to expect. There was no way to manage such an unfortunate catastrophic disease. **Sometimes experiences in life are the only preparation we get to help us through unexpected mishaps. It seems like incidents fall straight out of the sky and inundate our lives. Marene, 101.**

At the beginning of my husband's illness, we were in the prime of our lives. Curtis was only thirty four and I was thirty two. Our lovely daughters were all very young and school aged. I understood that both of us had chosen to marry and to give birth to those unsuspecting brats. However, we I did not drive up to the drive-thru window of life and order those distasteful experiences.

Polymyositis showed up in Curtis's muscles without a warning. That's how life is. Life didn't offer us an opportunity to prepare for set backs. They just happened to us and we had to buckle up our seat belts and deal with whatever came our way. There was no alternative to fold up or to give up. We were tossed around in life just like balls being juggled in the air. However, we had to step it up and work through the processes that life offered. We had suddenly been tossed into that "Field of Pain" without a survival kit. We could have whined until the cows came home, but that was not a part of our make up. Both of us chose to dive off into that arena of life, wrestle and fight back and survive. The funny thing was that we also had to throw our children into the arena and teach them how to fight life right along with us.

I had to immediately create a "Survival Kit" for my family and myself. My daddy had taught me since childhood that I was responsible for whatever happened to mein my own life and his words were becoming a reality in my life. Daddy also often said that, "If a man doesn't work, he ought not to eat." Again, he was right on point. Nobody owed us anything so we had to find a way to make it on our own. Choosing to run back home to mama and daddy was not our preference. My survival kit was going to fit right into the sizes of our experiences. I had to wrestle with the "bull's horns," and to let it swing me high and low and to make it happen on a daily basis.

It probably would've been nicer if we could've skipped a few days and nights so that the test could've been a little easier. Well, unfortunately, that was also not an option. When we got married and chose to have children therefore we accepted the responsibilities that went along with our decision. My husband hadn't asked to get sick and our children certainly didn't ask to be born. Therefore, I owed everybody the benefit of survival. My family deserved the best and I was going to see to it that we wouldn't have anything less than the best. In order for that to happen, I had to become the best at everything I did so I could influence the best for my family. I believed that with God and with faith on my side, I could achieve anything that I could imagine.

That nineteen years long experience was the catalyst that proved to mold me into the patient life student that I eventually became. Lessons learned from many of my experiences certainly provoked significant changes in our lives forever. Those lessons also conducted significant life growth and development for me. Ultimately, the brunt of that cycle rested on my shoulders. My husbands' illness was my hardest class in "Life's Lessons" and I had to constantly study and pray and learn how to navigate through those experiences and maintain my sanity. I was passing every test at the end of each "lesson" that life was invoking.

Yes, there were many nights of serious tears and questions. Sometimes I literally asked God questions on a daily basis like: Why me, Why this, and Why that? And, my life's teacher always responded with answers like, keep your faith and trust because there is something for you to learn from all this. Although, there were times when I felt like my life should've been a little easier. That was due in part to the fact that the weight of that responsibility rested primarily on my shoulders. Sometimes it seemed unbearable, but I hung in there and I kept a good attitude.

It is not easy to face life without the appropriate resources you need to survive. At one time, we experienced a seven month waiting period before we started getting significant help. We hardly knew what was going to happen to us from day to day. Back then the system was set up to serve people with normal hardships. If you had a less than normal situation, it could sometimes take the system longer to serve you which was exactly what happened to us. I made a conscientious decision to not complain about what was happening to us. Instead I chose to recognize the blessings that were occurring in our lives as a result of what was happening to us.

During that time we had very compassionate family, friends and church members that surrounded us like a band of angels. They stuck right by our sides and helped us all they could. My sister was an angel and so were all my four (4) brothers. I chose to try not to become a burden on people so I kept lots of stuff to myself. Whenever my sister visited me she always brought special gifts and goodies for me and the girls. She was always encouraging me and giving me advice. I so looked forward to seeing her!

I will also never forget how my friend Sally Mae who owned a beauty shop approached me after church one Sunday and told me that the Lord had told her to fix my hair. I felt a little embarrassed because I thought that maybe my hair looked badly or something. But she assured me that it had nothing to do with how my hair looked. She wanted to offer me free perms and enhance my present beauty. I was pregnant with my fifth child at that time. I accepted her offer not knowing that not only was she was going to fix my hair; she was also going to become a mentor and confidant to me. She was so kind and also full of wisdom and I started receiving something I never imagined.

Sally Mae taught me lessons while I was sitting her chair like; how to interact with certain people, especially those who agitated me. She was full of wisdom and taught me so much. I learned how to handle things in a very professional manner and how to become a virtuous woman. She was also very good at handling the usual politics that people deal with on a daily basis. There was one thing that I learned well and that was how to keep my mouth closed even when I knew that I was right. Her favorite quote was "It's better to be thought a fool than to open your mouth and remove all doubt." She taught me that some things are better left unsaid. Those were "life's lessons" for me that I still use to this day.

At first I felt confused, however, I learned to humble myself and listen to Sally. She had already been through many life trying experiences and she was willing to share information with me. Sometimes you can make it hard for someone to teach you when you pretend to know more than you really know. So, I listened to her and learned many things. Sally Mae was a very professional lady who knew how to carry herself. She was endowed with realness and lots common sense. I listened to her and I also learned some things from her by sheer observation. Then, when I eventually obtained a job, I carried her teachings with me to the job. She saved me from making many work and family mistakes that could have cost lots of pain for me in life. I didn't know at that time that I would eventually become the head of our household from a work perspective. Sally Mae became one of the angels in my life that helped me to grow and develop my career.

One of my closest girlfriends, Marcey, also stepped up during that time and helped me tremendously! She was such a source of inspiration and strength! Although she was quite younger than I, she was always encouraging, lifting me up, motivating me to push full speed ahead and look for my bright future. I found strength even in Marcey's voice, because she had an un-moveable faith in me and in God!

I was always amazed when new puzzle pieces mysteriously filled in the spaces of my life's arsenal. Things always worked out, shaped up and played out as beautiful lessons at the end of each experience! I rejoiced and gained more faith as I continued on. Faith was the only constant in my life at that time. My whole family's future was on life support and it was up to me to keep our future alive. I realized that my entire family's axis ledged on how I chose to handle situations. And, I chose to order some strength and mercy from above, and hang in there and not only survive but thrive!

People often expressed to me that they were inspired by the way I was handling things. That was how I maintained my positive energy and it attracted assistance as we went along. For example, specifically, one Christmas season our church surprised my family with an awesome Christmas! It seemed as if every member of that church bought our children something for xmas that year. We didn't have a clue that they were secretly gathering gifts for us. All of our girls received several dolls each, clothes, and much more than both my husband and I together could've provided for them on our income. We had so much stuff that I actually was able to share a few things with a few other unfortunate families. I believe that, **if you remain positive you can actually attract whatever you need into your world. Marene, 101.**

I learned how to draw upon my intellect. I had been raised well in my small sleepy town of Caruthersville, MO. I knew the golden rule, "always treat people the same way you want to be treated, work for what you get, and do without what you can to help yourself." **Sometimes people have a tendency to formulate erroneous ideas as to who is responsible for what has happened to them in life. Marene, 101.**

Chapter 5

Blackmanitis

May I now submit that every Black father is not absent in the African American home. I want to take a minute here and rant. Sometimes we get caught up in somebody else's issues and contend that all Black daddies are absent fathers. People have a tendency to accentuate the negative. I am the first to admit that my daddy was present in our home and he took the lead as the head of our house. He was a very sensitive, kind and sweet man who advocated for his wife, daughters and all women. He taught his sons how to treat women with his very life as he demonstrated while treating our mama with respect. Listen, we were going to respect mama and that was that!

I can also remember all the pats on the back and boost ups that I received from my daddy when I was a little girl. He continued this practice even after I was grown and married. After having my children I still could sit on my daddy's knee and chat with him.

I want to be the one to let the world know that there has always been good black daddy's. My daddy's leadership played a major role in how I would respond to conflict and adversity in my life. He was always saying things like; "Girl, you can do this!" And, I well up with tears as I look back and think about how many times daddy said to me when I was crying about something, "Now come on, be a big girl!" He would wrap his arms around me and sit me on his knee and teach me how to face life.

Daddy was a fearless outspoken protective father and the leader of our family. We didn't have to hear anything about an absent father. Daddy was alive and well, setting rules and he remained ready to enforce broken rules when he needed to. He had a very serious back up plan! I contend that he was not the only good black man.

Don't get me wrong, I remain very sensitive and loyal to the many single moms that exist in our society. I also understand and recognize that many women and men have had to raise families alone. However, I humbly contend, that all black men are not irresponsible. That very statement is a stereotype that needs to be changed in our mind-sets. There have been countless black men who have stuck by their wives, raised their own children as single fathers and many men have worked their fingers to the bone to deliver strong family units back into our society.

Thus, my story is just a little different from the single parent's perspective. The last thing I want to convey in this book is another case of Blackmanitis. I applaud all the black men as well as all other fathers who have put their hands to the grinding stones of life and passed the torch on to another healthy family structure. That's always a significant benefit to our society! I want to give rise to a different concept of black men and all men that take responsibility, and there are many. I think that the numbers are higher on the positive side. My daddy's love and instructions gave me the strength and confidence I needed to step up to the plate and take the lead in my home when responsibilities mandated.

Because of such strong teachings from my father I remained respectful to the fact that my husband was the man of our household. Howbeit, he was ill and someone had to feed the babies. Thus, I enrolled in a local community college with the intentions of being a better help mate to him and fate made a quick switch in our lives. Eventually, we had to change roles and I became the breadwinner in our home.

Prior to my husband's terminal illness we were the average couple involved in life and living a normal life. Our girls were growing up and things were very stable in our lives. Our eldest daughter was a self taught musician for a local church. Her talent brought in a little income for her that served well in enhancing her ability to learn to assume responsibility for herself. Since she was the oldest girl she was already serving as a role model for her sisters. She was demonstrating how personal talent could pay off when used correctly. She was also learning the art of working for what she got in life. You see, life is always teaching lessons.

Another one of our daughters eventually landed an excellent job at a local hospital, even while she was in high school. She later graduated from an Ivy League college and eventually became the first girl in our family to obtain a master's degree and to date; two of our five daughters have obtained their master's degrees.

Then, another daughter also worked at Sears while in high school and she worked for one of our closest friends cleaning house on Saturdays. They also helped her in many other ways. Not to mention that my other two daughters eventually worked also while they were still in high school.

I was also endowed with lots of natural talent. People often called me an "idea machine." I had a special gift of creating things and improvising, networking, innovating and finding ways to make things work out. I also worked several jobs at a time which brought in various streams of income. With the size family Curtis and I had; it took lots of work to make ends meet. I learned how to supplement our small income by picking up cans and bottles and selling them and I was also seamstress. Additionally, I made crafts, cabbage patch dolls, home decoration items and also sold them. I was very artful with flower arrangements and other crafty things. I also had a special gift with green house plants. My hands were blessed hands! And I learned to "Use what I had," to work with. I was always creating something for our survival. There wasn't any time set aside for us to feel intimidated or sad. We were going to become successful in our own rites!

Our daughters formed a singing group called "The Austin Sisters," when they were still very young. Our oldest daughter was their musician. I will never forget the time when the pastor's wife at our church solicited our daughters to be "Mystery Guest" at one of our church's evening services. After the announcement was made about this, parishioners were seeking info on who would be the mystery guest and I had to pretend that I also didn't know what they were talking about. Then, it was very funny when the Austin Sisters stepped up at that service once the Mystery Guest was introduced.

Things like that helped us to keep our girls grounded, busy and off the streets. When they were not in school or at church, they were practicing for a singing engagement. Don't get me wrong, they were regular children and were just like other girls. They also made some of the same mistakes as anyone else. We had average teenagers and we consistently enforced our rules. They had rules, directions and guidelines whether or not they abided by them. We tried to keep them out of devilment. For the most, part some of our daughters graduated high school in the upper percentile of their classes. All of them went to college, and two out of five obtained master's degrees.

Sometimes people fall on hard times and life lends us mandates to maintain and deal with our difficulties. Life also teaches us the lessons to be learned from each one of our experiences. When life shows up carrying an arsenal of training you can chose to cope and succeed or we can croak, and fail. Marene, 101.

There we were, on our journey in life with no idea of what to expect from day to day. At times, we had little to no income. We didn't have health or life insurance available to us. My husband was obviously facing the end of his life. As life would design it we learned that my husband was ill only one month after I had already enrolled in a community college. I was all excited because I had decided to finally begin to develop my career after motherhood, then Curtis became ill. Now, we were experiencing this big bump in the road of our lives. In addition to my college classes, life added another class called "Adversity."

While Curtis was terminally ill, and while I was in school, life induced an additional school called "The school of hard knocks." I didn't have a job at that time and my husband was only working periodically at his carpenter job. Already, we could barely make ends meet, and now this. The rent had to be paid, the utility bill was a constant, not to mention the challenges of all the other bills and obligations, and there was no consistent income to accommodate us.

In the meantime, Curtis kept getting sick and sicker. We had to support our family and also educate our children. So, what do you do, when life's lights are cut off without a cutoff notice? I had already been taught in my upbringing how to survive. Now, life would test that knowledge to the core. In my mind, becoming a loser was not a preference and quitting college never entered the equation. I had to press on and endure. I was all we had at the time. Consequently, I jumped into the ring and fought life back with both fists! That was my "choice!" I decided to take the upper road and grab the bull's horns. My motto was, "I could, or I would die trying." Everyday when I got in that old car to drive myself to school or work, I would tell myself that "there is a way and I was going to find it." What did I have to lose, and, I had so much to gain. Sink or swim, I had a choice.

Chapter 6

Sometimes it simply takes a miracle

Often there were overwhelming utility bills and many cut off notices. Many times our services were actually cut off because I did not always make enough money to meet their requirements. Sometimes when our lights were off, we took advantage of the sunlight and did our homework on the front porch before night. Then I would put the children to bed early. That way we I could hide the fact that there were no services. Sometimes you can keep girls from talking too much. I was amazed at how they were still honor roll students right in the middle of all our hardships. Faith and determination was really working for us! We consistently witnessed miracles on a daily bases.

While driving to school one day in my old hoopty I was very concerned because there I was once again, driving on empty without gas money. That was such a scary feeling! But, what the heck, I had to take the chance and go on to school. Again, I was leaning on my faith to get me through. Then a thought came to me. My inner voice spoke to me and told me to turn in at a local service station. This incident happened doing the time when service station attendants pumped gas and washed windshields for their customers. When the attendant came to my cracked window and asked me how much gas I wanted, I responded with, "The Lord said give me some gas." To my surprise he obeyed. "Okay," he said, then, he proceeded to pump gas into my tank. I felt somewhat weird and I thought to myself that maybe he didn't understand what I had said to him. When he finished pumping my gas, he came back to my window and said, "You can go now!" I left the station slowly as I glared through my rear view mirror, saying to myself, "Wow, was that an angel?" At first, I was glaring through the back windshield wondering if someone would soon be chasing me down. I could not stop thinking about that incident so when I got my paycheck, I went back to the service station and offered to repay the attendant for that wonderful favor. The last thing I wanted to do was to take advantage of someone. But he replied, "No you are not going to pay me anything back!" "I can remember my grandmamma from back in the day when she used to testify in church," he said. "She was always telling people about how God would send angels to help her when she could barely make it." **Nothing surprises God, and sometimes he creates experiences so that we can recognize his realness and learn lessons on how to trust him to take care of us. Marene, 101.**

The entire time that I was in college, as well as, throughout my career, I was challenged with my husband's illness and taking care of the family. We experienced countless hospital stays and intensive care scares. A few times he was given up on by some of his physicians. He certainly was battling the bouts with that muscle disease. That experience was very stressful. I really needed and wanted to work but without adequate skills my job search remained limited. Therefore, I stuck to my personal talents of making and selling dolls, crafts and cans and bottles while working odd jobs.

One day when I was attending college and sitting in my Anatomy and Physiology class, Dr. Purreal, who was head of the Science Department at Shelby State Community College, was teaching our class that day. After roll call he looked at me and said, "Marene, I want to see you right after class today." Oh, God, I thought, what could he want with me! So reluctantly, I went to see him at the end of my class and to my surprise, he asked me if I wanted a job. Without hesitation, I said, "YES!" Then, he said, "I want you to start working for me in the Science Lab. I need another Lab Assistant." I became extremely excited! That was another miracle! I rushed home that evening jumping, shouting and laughing. I called everybody that I could think of and told them my exciting news. Now, I will get a check every two weeks and I will be able to better support my family. I was beginning to see purpose and started saying, "things were truly going to work out for me."

Additionally, we also were approved to receive welfare and food stamps soon afterwards. At that time my case was delayed because I was married which required a little more research before approval. Things were looking up for us. That was a means to an end. I was already working towards improving our lives and self-sufficiency. I had to do what I had to do. We were starting to see how things would workout if we kept on trying. My load was getting a little lighter because we had started to make more progress. I started feeling good about making small accomplishments! **If you try you can improve your circumstances. Never give up! Everything that's happening in your life is getting you closer to your goal. It's like a small drop of water from the sky is a sign of rain even when the evidence is contradictory. Marene, 101.**

I made a commitment to myself to be the best Lab Assistant that Dr. Purreal had ever seen. I was very motivated and full of energy! Both my mama and daddy had taught me to be the best that I could be at everything that I attempted to do in life.

My new job description was to dissect cats in the science lab. Those cats were being studied by the students in all Science classes like Anatomy & Physiology, Biology and Microbiology, etc. They were learning to identify nerves, muscles, arteries, and vessels. I was also a student and studied while working which gave me an edge. I looked at that opportunity as another puzzle piece being filled in by life.

When I first started working in the science department, I felt beleaguered looking at all those lifeless cats. I constantly swallowed and took deep breaths to make mental adjustments. A part of my job was to prep cats for lab studies and I had to learn how to become the best at it. My personal coping mechanism was to become familiar with each one of my cats and make them my personal friends. They all had their own identity, colors, strips, spots and weight. I gave each one of them a name and talked to them while working on them and setting up the lab. That activity made me feel a little better about dissecting my cats. It started seeming to not be so bad after all.

A few months after I started working in the science lab, my supervisor went on medical leave. Within a couple weeks again, Dr. Purreal called me in his office and told me that he was going to assign me to work in my boss's position while she was out. There were about fourteen lab assistants and I had been favored to lead the team. I accepted his offer with joy! Then he gave me the keys to her office. I was very excited and thankful! In the next few days I was busy cleaning the office because it was in disarray. You know, like giving it the Marene's touch. That was such an act of innocence on my part. Little did I know that I was about to get my first serious lesson in office politics.

When my supervisor returned to work from sick leave and observed all the changes, she became very angry at me. I couldn't understand why she was mad because she knew that the boss had made that assignment. Nevertheless, she came into the office and told me, "You ain't no supervisor here." "It's only going to be one supervisor in this office, and that's me." "Do you understand me, Marene?" I was stunned! "You'd better get back over there and start back to working in your little lab assistant position, if you know what's good for you." I didn't know what to do. I didn't want it to seem as though I couldn't handle working with people so I kept this to myself hoping it would work itself out. I wanted to process that office political move like a grown woman. So, I simply ignored her and kept doing my job. **You can find bullies everywhere like work, church, school and sometimes in family settings. Marene, 101.**

Then again, early one morning, while we were alone in the lab my office bully (former boss) approached me again. She meant to make her command stick in my mind this time. I felt vulnerable because I was really trying to let my personality work this issue out. I had no other defense.

I certainly did not want to get into any trouble and I really needed to work. I had a family to feed and I was not going to sacrifice them because she could not deal with her insecurity. I kept my mouth closed and took the flack. My demeanor made her feel powerful, so she proceeded to continually intimidate me. This time, she took her first finger and put it on my nose and pushed it in, and said, "do you understand me Marene!?" "There will be only one supervisor in this lab, and that's me, Marene! "Do you understand me?" I really felt her passion and anger, but I also knew that was not the origin of her pain. "You can get your butt back in your role as a lab assistant, do you hear me?" Again, I didn't respond to her. **Being silent and keeping your mouth closed doesn't necessarily prove that you are guilty or ignorant, it can sometimes prove that you are peaceful and don't want to add value to the foolishness of others. Marene 101.**

By then, I felt my feathers ruffle a little. She was taking chances and going just a little too far this time. But, I was in full control of myself. I didn't have any problems, I thought. And I was happily working, drawing a check every two weeks and taking care of my family. Nobody was going to interfere with my personal progress. Therefore, I pressed my lips together and inwardly gritted my teeth, took a deep breath and spoke very calmly to her. "Betty, please take your hand out of my face." She was acting in total disrespect but I had to be strong for my family. I could not let her win, so I went inside myself and said quietly, "HELP ME LORD." I won that fight with my maturity! Don't get me wrong, I felt tremendous emotional pain from her childish actions. However, I was not going to participate in a cat fight confrontation that could cause me to lose my job or my reputation. I didn't say another word to her and went on and continued doing my job. I CHOSE peace! I was in full control of me because I had a vision for my life, and she was not going to break my spirit or destroy my dream.

I had to think . . . FAST! I am at work to provide for my family. Why should I get involved in someone else's issue? I could not and would not play into her political jealousy. She wanted to control me so she could feel power. In the meantime, I was doing what my boss had told me to do. I felt that if she disagreed with his decisions, then, she should be discussing that with him and not with me. Betty would just have to make this adjustment to change on her own, I thought. I was okay with the change. I was not responsible for a decision that management had made and implemented. That wheel had been turned while she was off from work. My allegiance was to my boss, not to my co-worker. Therefore, I kept a cool head and put up with her until this could be officially resolved by management.

Needless to say, that situation made me feel very sad! So, when I got a moment to myself I decided to walk down the hall to the storage room and cool off and make a mental adjustment. I really wanted to feel better over that whole situation. When I got to the storage room I sat down and cried softly to myself. I felt a little broken up over all of that foolishness! Quietly, I asked the Lord, WHY? Why was I being violated by a work bully, and how should I handle the situation? I asked. I had my normal personal pity party. Then, I thought about how nice I had been to her and all my coworkers. I got along with everybody and now she comes back to work starting mess. I would lament! But, while I was crying, I remembered a message that I had once heard from a former pastor, "Don't ever let the devil see you cry." Uh, I thought, I am going to wash my face and go back to the work area with a positive attitude. I don't have to be sad over this or anything else. I chose strength!

Then, just at that time I had a Muse. My inner voice spoke to me and said, "Baby, dry your tears." "It's time for you to move on. This is the beginning of a new chapter in your life." While that thought sounded good in my mind, I didn't have a clue as to where this new chapter might be taking me but the thought sounded very good and positive. Therefore, I reacted as if I knew where I was going, and I obeyed my inner voice. I was beginning to witness another new chapter in my life and I was wise enough to recognize that God's will for me was taking me places. I needed to turn the page and move on.

My inner voice proceeded to say, "You go back down there and tell them that you have a job at Federal Express." That thought really felt and sounded good. I felt good in my spirit and I believed and acted on it. That move was about faith. I had never applied for a job at Federal Express neither did I know where the company was located at that time.

However, I thought, I need to speak that idea into existence! It won't cost me anything to believe. Suddenly, I became very excited and rushed back to the work area and announced to all my co-workers that I had a job at Federal Express and that I would be leaving in a few days. While I was feeling so confident I went on and announced that there would be a going away party in two weeks. As I spoke by faith, the more everything seemed to become real in my spirit. I also actually pictured the job becoming a reality in my mind. People believed me and we all were excited and looking forward to my going away party. The word was getting out and I was getting feedback like: WHAT? WHEN? HOW DID YOU DO THAT?

Boy was I having fun! Everybody in the department was excited with me and some people even joined in and started inviting staff from other departments to the going away party. Some people even volunteered to pot luck and bring food dishes while others contributed cash for the party. Then I proceeded with my plans for my departure from Shelby State. Later I submitted a two weeks notice to my boss. I hugged him and told him how much I appreciated working for him and thanked him for all he had done in extending many on the job opportunities to me. I thanked him for believing in me and told him how much I had learned while working in the Science Lab. I had also started working in the Lab Supervisor's position without any formal leadership skills, yet with a little training I had successfully led a team of fourteen Lab Assistants.

Dr. Purreal also joined the excitement in preparation for my celebration! He complimented me and even gave me a letter of recommendation to take to my new boss. He said that he really understood why I had to make such a decision. Finally, he admitted to me that he had already made a decision to cut my hours from twenty to ten hours a week. He wished me well! **You never know why adversity is happening in your life. Sometimes adversity is preparing you to try on the shoes that will carry you to and through your next steps in life's lessons. Marene, 101.**

Something was still missing in that picture. There I was celebrating a position at Federal Express that I had never applied for. Furthermore, I didn't even know where the company was located. I had heard lots of good things about Federal Express but at that time I had not looked into working for the company. I also knew a few people who worked there, but what was I doing? I thought. All that excitement really made me feel exuberant and my inner voice was in agreement with the way things were going. I had no other choice but to believe! There was something about believing, having faith and speaking things into existence that resonated in my spirit. That process truly worked for me. My faith was about the things that I believed in but I could not see them with my natural eyes. **"That was a spiritual awakening for me, a MUSE."**

Chapter 7

Believing in Faith Became a Life Choice

My assignment was finished at the community college. I had grown to the max in that job and I continued to grow in my career. I was going to have to learn how to change myself into larger "life clothes." It was time for me to move on. **The spirit can see things way before we can even visualize or sometimes even think about them. It's kind of like a parent preparing a child for the next grade in school or bigger chores at home. Marene, 101.** I could actually look out there on the horizon and see how that move was going to enhance my career growth. I had the right to "believe in what I believed in." Gleefully, I prepared for my going away party and my move to Federal Express. Ultimately, my going away party was very upbeat and joyful! Everybody was happy for me and I was getting a great new job by faith and now my faith had lot's more work to do!

My inner voice spoke to me again and told me to prepare a resume and to take it to church that upcoming Sunday and give it to Alex Adams after the church service. I asked our Secretary at the college if she would please help me to prepare a professional resume for my new job. She looked at me real funny and said; "I thought you already had this job." And, I said, "I do so let's do the resume and move on."

That Sunday after church, I hand delivered my resume to Alex Adams who was already a manager at Federal Express. Initially, he refused to take my resume, apologized and explained that he could not make any management referrals at that time. He explained that the company had put a hold on referrals. He explained to me that they had stopped about a week prior. I was one week too late. Respectfully, I took my resume back and started walking towards my car. Then my inner voice spoke to me again and said, "I told you to give it to Alex." I stopped and ran back across the parking lot to Alex's car and said, "Alex, you've got to take this resume. It's up to you what you do with it, but, I have got to give it to you." So, Alex took the resume and said, "OK." Then, on their way home from church that evening he and his wife, Marcey, were discussing how they could help me when Alex suddenly came up with a bright idea.

After I got home that evening I received a phone call from Alex. *"Marene, we have thought about a way to get you on at Federal Express.* Just sit tight and I will call you later." Then, I looked up and said, "Thank you Jesus!" Alex and his wife were both impressed with my perseverance and faith. So, I just waited and waited, and waited patiently to receive my call from Alex.

I waited and waited and waited until four weeks had passed. All that time I had to keep the faith. I wouldn't let anybody discourage me from believing that I would receive a call for my new job. While I waited, I prepared my attitude and mind for work. I knew that I would get that job. My faith was all I had to hold on to. And I had a right to believe anything I wanted to. I was so amazed at how that voice had so forcefully told me that I would be getting a job at Federal Express even when I was still working at the college.

Then, one day at about 1:00 p.m. Alex called me and said, "Marene, how long will it take you to get out here?" I became very excited! It's the job, I thought. "Just give me a few minutes, I replied, "and I will be there," I said. My car was down at the time and I didn't even have enough money to ride the city bus. However, I knew one thing for sure and it was that there was no way that I was going to receive this much anticipated call and not show up for that job. Things had to work out for me! I had to keep my faith in the moment! Then, I stepped out on my front porch desperately looking both ways up and down my street when I noticed that one of my neighbors, Mr. Frazier, was sitting, on his front porch. He was about eighty two years old and I didn't know if he was still driving, but I rushed down to his house and said, "Mr. Frazier, could you please give me a ride out to Federal Express so I can get a job?" And, he responded, "Sure ma'am, let me get my cap." I didn't have any idea of how I was going to get back home that day, but first things first here. I needed to get to the job first! I needed a ride to Federal Express and I had a ride to Federal Express. **When you want something you have to develop an appetite for it and then keep right on searching and believing until you find it. Marene, 101.**

Needless to say, what really happened was very non-traditional. A vacancy had been created at the Switchboard in the Hub just for me. The existing Switchboard Operator was out sick and they needed a dependable Switchboard Operator. There I was ready and willing to fill that vacancy. All I had to do was to sit down and talk on the phone. Oh my God, what a break, can things get any easier, I loved talking on the phone! That was my favorite thing to do. Alex needed me to start working right there on the spot. He told me to sit at the Switchboard for my first four hour shift. "After you finish your shift I will bring you in and then we can do your hiring paperwork."

Immediately I did what I was told and became a FedEx Hub Switchboard Operator on the spot. I was so excited! I didn't know what the heck I was doing or talking about, but I was faking it right through the process. I made it up as I went along. I was also still attending school at the local college at that time. I just made whatever adjustments I needed to make. That's the way it is. You work around the job. In most cases, jobs are not customized to fit your lifestyle. You get in compliance and adjust to the job. I was not turning down anything here. This opportunity is going to make life better for me and my family, I thought.

I sat right there and worked the next four hours and answered the phones like I was told to do. Then, when it was time for me to go home, I thought,

Lord, how will I get home? I didn't know anyone at the company at the time. I knew that I was going to have to be creative in getting myself back home. Federal Express was a long way from my house and, remember, I still didn't have bus fare! What am I going to do? I thought to myself. How was I going to get back home and furthermore, how was I going to get back out there the next day? Oh well, I thought, let life fill in the puzzle pieces here. I've got the job so this is definitely going to work out for me, I had to believe and keep the faith!

To my surprise when I got back outside Mr. Frazier was still out there sitting in his car waiting for me. I ran over to his car and said, "Oh my God, Mr. Frazier, I didn't know that you were going to wait for me!" I laughed out loud, "I can't believe this!" And, he replied, "Well you told me to bring you out here and you never came back out here and told me what to do next, so I just waited for you." Wow, I thought, what a blessing!

When we returned home, I thanked him and asked him how much I owed him, and he said, "There is no charge." Then he said, "I have noticed how hard you work and how hard you are trying to support your family." "I am just glad to be able to help you ma'am!" Then, he continued to drive me back and forth to work for a few days until my husband fixed my ole car. **Life always cooperates with you when you cooperate with life. Marene, 101.**

There I was, now working at Federal Express, a Switchboard Operator, learning skills as I went along. To think, I didn't even have to compete for this job because the spirit said that I would be getting a job at Federal Express while I was still working at the college and I BELIEVED that with all my heart and acted on my faith. I was definitely counting my blessings and I was not going to take anything or anybody for granted. That was a real miracle for me. God is always good! I must continue to do my part like believing and acting on what he speaks to me through my inner voice. **I believe that when a door opens you need to rush in while it is still open. Marene, 101.** My life was shaping up because I was trying very hard to succeed and my life's puzzle pieces were falling right in place.

I worked at the switchboard one full year while I consistently prepared myself for my next step. In the meantime, I graduated from Shelby State Community College and received my 1st degree after fifteen years of marriage and five babies. My oldest daughter also graduated from high school around that same time. She was my inspiration!

While working at the switchboard I also continued taking various educational classes because I knew that there was more out there on the horizon for me. I wanted to prepare myself for a full time position at the company. Therefore, again I enrolled in a technical school so as to enhance my marketable skill set and to become more promotable. My degree was in Radiologic Technology and I needed to sharpen my office technology, interpersonal, and data entry skills. Thus, I took the appropriate continuing education classes. At that time, I had only worked in healthcare at various hospitals and clinics. At that point my career was moving me in a different direction. I learned that working in an office environment and interacting with people was a much better match with my "butterfly personality." I fit right into that type of work environment. I loved working in customer service and communicating with various people every day.

I had worked very hard in the last two years in an attempt to finish college and I was delighted that I had accomplished so much. Then my self esteem and self confidence started soaring through the roof. Not to mention that, I was still challenged with my husband's illness and being a working mom.

From time to time my mama came to Memphis and spent a few days with me to help ease the heavy load that I bearing. I had great family support and that also served to help me to succeed and to give me added emotional support.

Lots of days after dinner I had to help our girls with their homework before I could even think about doing my own homework. My husband also helped them whenever he could. I made sure that my husband was being taken care of. Sometimes after leaving work and school, I would also drop by the hospital and visit my husband from time to time whenever he was hospitalized and that was often. Then, I had to get home to the five girls and take care of them. That was my role as a working mother. Many times, I would end up studying all night after everybody else was fast asleep. Circumstances in life did not avert me from my own responsibilities and sunrise became one of my constant companions.

Life was very intense at that time and I had to cultivate a rhythm that would work for all of us. That was Life and I had to deal with it. Faith was my greatest possession! I had to hold on to something greater than me that would continually propel me to and through my next steps. I read the Bible, meditated, prayed daily and attended church services. I had little time for leisure in my life at that time. That process also helped me to deal with all the awesome responsibilities that were incumbent upon me. Additionally, I kept my children involved in church and other activities. That's how we found the spiritual strength to continue on and remain positive. I believed in faith like I believed in breathing and I used my faith to the max.

As I started to grow in my career, I spent countless hours reading books and participating in self help activities. When I took my children to the public library, I often used that time to check out countless books and videos that could also enhance my own educational growth. I learned to spend my spare time on positive profiling instead of complaining and blaming. **You actually can do much more in a day than you think you can if you subtract the negative elements. So cherish every moment that you get and then insert yourself into the slots of time. Marene, 101.**

The following four months I took a business class at a technical school called Data Control Institute. At that time I was challenged with child care because I couldn't afford to pay someone to babysit for me. My baby girl was only fifteen months old at the time. One day when I was explaining my dilemma to one of my best girl friends, she took it upon herself to accommodate me. She always told me that she admired my dedication and determination. So, she offered to keep my baby everyday while I was in school. I didn't know at the time that she was battling breast cancer. I accepted her offer and finished my eighteen months class in four months. I didn't want to run my welcome out so I converted my two day four hours a day classes into five days a week eight hours a day. That way, I could complete my classes in less time and I was successful at that. Aretha Bradley (God rest her soul) volunteered to keep my baby. She took good care of and spoiled my baby. She refused to discuss money and said that she wanted to do me a favor and help me out. **People will help you when they see you trying to help yourself. Marene, 101.** I considered that as another one of my greatest blessings because Aretha already had nine children of her own. Upon finishing those classes, I later applied for and was promoted to a full time position on the corporate side at Federal Express in the Invoice Adjustments Department.

Again, I was elated! There I was again, calling people, testifying about my new accomplishment! Some of the perks that came with that opportunity were life and health insurance, dental insurance, vision, educational reimbursements and travel and shipping discounts for my entire family. Things were certainly looking up for us. I was very grateful for all this! I was starting to navigate through life like an experienced boatman. I was enjoying participating in the opportunities that life was offering me, and I was slowly progressing!

My entire family, did all they could to help me and I still was strapping trying to help myself. Family members, close friends and some of my church members constantly called me and encouraged me on a daily basis. They have remained my cheerleaders to this day. **People love good stories and people love helping people who are trying very hard to help themselves. Marene, 101.** By then, I had become an Invoice Adjustment Agent at Federal Express. The things that I was able to learn in that position kind of made it feel like I was actually taking another life class.

Chapter 8

The Class of Life and Success

I received lots of training that served to mold me into the professional that I eventually became. **Let's call this the class of Life and Success.** There are many chilly winds of adversity that go along with success and learning. It seems like one would be wise to recognize this fact up front. The politics along that came with working in corporate became life changing for me; not to mention all the new learning experiences that I would also receive.

Once I became acclimated in the corporate office the pace of the games picked up speed. I was already somewhat accustomed to games, but games took another shape in corporate and I was not ready. I had to learn quickly and respond quicker because the game was almost over when I would recognize that a game was in operation in the office. I had to learn how to block it before it got to the forefront and hurt me. Those new office games came with unique techniques and life experiences were my only teachers. Sometimes the rules of the games seemed to change every hour.

I had to be ready to win those office games or I was not going to make it. That fact required me to keep my thinking cap on all day long. Those were games that "mama certainly never taught me." It became very intricate just to stay out of trouble. For example, I was placed in a mostly complacent work group of office employees whom it seemed that their greatest interest was payday. I observed that some of those people were sometimes finding excuses not to work. Case in point, I noticed how sometimes people would pick up a clean sheet of paper and walk over to someone else's cubicle and use the paper as a cloak to gossip. They would appear to be discussing something pertaining to work. They were busy alright, spreading rumors and gossip in the office and those same people were always complaining when someone else were recognized for a job well done.

One time I returned to my desk from the bathroom and while I was away, someone had dropped stacks of their paperwork on my desk. When I left, I was caught up on my paperwork and they were jealous because I was always ahead of them in my work. Well, I see it this way, if you are consistently working you are prone to get more work done than someone who is messing off on the job. I worked hard to catch up on my own work but they were playing and using my fast paced skills to their own advantage. I could turn my head and a bundle of someone else's work would appear on my desk. I had to watch out for myself and stay ready to fight like a political wild animal. They were just not going to sit there and allow someone to come in that department and out shine everybody else. That was like an "Office initiation butt kicking."

Its double for your trouble, if you thought that you were going to be an "Office energizer bunny," like I was. One day, two of my coworkers approached me and asked me to slow my pace. They said that I was taking too many calls and processing too much paperwork. "You make us (the rest of the workgroup) look bad," they said. They took the time and explained to me in a very nice manner that I was working too hard. I took their suggestion very lightly and just smiled and shrugged them off. Then, the next thing I knew I saw the two of them in our manager's office talking to her. I never knew what they told her, but after that day, my supervisor turned on me. She started watching my every move and critiquing everything I did. Every time anything happened in the department, she basically addressed it with me first, then the rest of the group. Sometimes l didn't even know what she was talking about. To think, prior to that incident, I was always getting compliments and award letters from my boss. What happened?

Well, that triggered me to dig deeper and work even harder if I planned to succeed in that department. They were not going to define me or influence my destiny. I still knew who I was and I was absolutely not going to change. I kept right on working very hard, as a matter of fact, I picked up my pace a little just to agitate them and I continued to excel in the department. My biggest concern was my own job evaluation. I knew that if I looked good on paper I would be prepared for the next move no matter what they said or thought about me. It was my responsibility to choose my own future career. **Adversity eventually fades away as you work your way through issues and shine. Marene, 101.**

I maintained my same philosophy of being the best that I could be at everything I did. I was happy to have that job. The benefits along motivated me! I knew what was important to me. I couldn't forget how God had blessed me with my job. So I continued to arrive at work at least thirty minutes early everyday. Sometimes I was there waiting for someone to open the building so I could get in there and start working. I didn't know that there was such a thing as being late or absent from work. That food was looking good on the table for my family and I was not going to sacrifice my career advancement for complacent coworkers who didn't even seem to have goals of their own. My positive attitude seemed to cause people to feel uneasy around me. I was singled out and some people were always complaining about everything that I did. It certainly seemed to be that way.

I was moved from Invoice Adjustments to the Billing Service Center. While that was a lateral move, I still was happily working in the corporate Billing Service Center (Critical Customer Service) and it seemed like I literally brought energy to work with me everyday! I was very positive, focused and driven! I loved all of this! I was happy to be in charge of my own life. Sometimes at lunch time I would take a health walk around the complex. That helped me to focus, maintain my stability and stress level.

Walking also gave me more energy and a boost that got me through the rest of the evening. Nobody had a clue as to what I was dealing with at home everyday.

Sometimes people don't like it when you can stand up and stand alone without the fear of controversy or rejection. Marene, 101. They simply can't understand where your motivation comes from. They know that most people won't even have anything to do with you and are also talking about you and you can still wear a smile! WOW! That kind of attitude can sometimes create envy towards a person in the work area and in life.

In the meantime, I became an expert at solving complex customer complaints in my department. People often called from other departments and specifically asked to speak with me. That was due mostly in part to the fact that I had developed a good reputation for solving customer complaints. I was very knowledgeable in company policies and procedures because I studied my work and I worked hard to retain customers for the company. I was pretty proficient in resolving and closing complaints. **How well you do your work is really what counts at the end of the day also what counts on your job evaluation. Marene, 101.** I would even take the time and complete my work even if it took me several days to process. I loved working and I loved the type of work that I was doing. It allowed me to meet people on the phone everyday. In my imagination I was visiting different cities as I talked to various people all over the world. I felt that I had taken a secret vacation. I felt a sense of accomplishment when I left a satisfied customer at the end of a call. **There is good in everything if you take out the time and look for it. Marene, 101.**

I also loved the challenge of figuring out various ways to solve customer's complaints. If I was required to walk over the building or to leave my floor in order to research a complaint, I was willing to do that also if I needed to. I was always willing to get the job done. Eventually, I developed a niche' in customer service and became an expert. I welcomed difficult complaints because in working those complex complaints; I learned new techniques and I ended up developing special skills to solve difficult problems. That attitude caused me to receive many awards and accolades in the department. It seemed to me that most people were spending too much of their time complaining and finding fault. I noticed that they didn't seem very happy. Some of those people could take an accomplishment down to its lowest common denominator.

Chapter 9

Learn How to Extract Knowledge
out of the Experience

*E*verything you learn in life does not necessarily come from a classroom or text book. Life has a way of setting up a make shift classroom almost anywhere or everywhere. Life experiences afforded me lots of much needed exposure and served as my personal training camp. I was learning how to deal with difficult situations and difficult people who would eventually end up out there in that "Field of Pain" that I had dreamed about.

Ultimately, I needed to learn how to solve problems because helping people solve problems was going to eventually become my life's work. I would eventually get into that work, and I would be confident in the fact that through the exposure I had obtained on my job, I would be able to easily find the right solutions and not become beset by complexities.

I was so involved in my work that it never occurred to me that I was exceeding all my departments' expectations. My name was always at the top on the status reports. That work ethic helped me to stand out in the department in the eyes of management. Thus, management often referred to me as a model employee! Eventually, I was chosen to train other employees and also to teach customer service techniques in my department. I simply remained available and open to any and all opportunities that came my way. As I grew in my career my pleasant attitude continued paying off for me.

I took every opportunity to work overtime hours whenever it was offered. My idea of working over time was synonymous to working two jobs while remaining at the same location. Staying on location saved on gas and time. Then, I was getting paid time and a half for working overtime. To me, that equated to a highly paid second job. Not to mention how much personal energy I was saving while remaining on site.

I continually set new goals and benchmarks for myself. I made a pledge to compete with myself at work. Status quo was not an option for me. I had to continually grow as I improved in productivity. Every week I compelled myself to increase in the number of calls that I took each day. Needless to say, I started exceeding work standards and expectations. That made me more marketable for advancement in the company. I was always seeking to improve my performance and my attitude. Eventually I was processing over two hundred calls a day versus the standard eighty five calls a day. I was breaking records and constantly setting new benchmarks. I guess you know how many people stayed mad at me at work, especially the lazy people. Eventually a co-worker named me "Motor Mouth," Ha, Ha!

I was very focused and driven so it took me a little while to figure out that some people were plotting and trying to cause me to fail. On one unassuming day, my manager called me in her office and asked me what time was I arriving at work daily. I was somewhat puzzled over the nature of her question because while I was a salaried employee that was not required to clock in before starting to work; I still figured that the company had a system that tracked our start time on the computer. She continued in her accusation stating, "I was told that you are lying about your time, Marene." During that period of time as salaried employees we were required to document our time on paper. However, I had a backup system where I would also sign in on the computer when I arrived at work everyday. She was implying that I was falsifying my timesheets and that didn't set very well with me. That was a cause for serious concern because that accusation was a play on my integrity! After research on my computer system records, I actually was able to prove through documentation that I was actually starting my day earlier than my papers documented. For some reason, I had a habit of signing in on the computer before I did anything else everyday and that paid off for me in documenting my start time. Those computer records certainly took my integrity back up a notch. That particular time their accusations actually made me look good! And, to think, they meant it for evil. Later, my boss went back and tracked the unaccounted time on the computer and then she reimbursed me for the unreported time.

It was always something. Some people even lied and said that I was cheating on my phone calls. They claimed that the reason that I was taking so many calls was that I knew how to count my dropped calls, although the system was counting the calls. The next thing I knew, my boss started monitoring my calls, and again, they were proven wrong. My work was constantly being scrutinized and audited by some of management and also some of my over zealous coworkers. I thought to myself, if they would do their own darn jobs they wouldn't have so much time to always mess with my job and maybe they too could take more calls. They were never able to find anything on me. My work was proven authentic and genuine.

Another example is, when I was a new agent in the Billing Service Center, it seemed like my co-workers bullied me and tried to second guess most of my decisions. I would go to work everyday and try to do the best job that I could do and that kept me pumped up. Some people thought that it was strange for me to mind my own business and work hard and excel. I was never standing around talking and keeping up with office gossip. They were always talking over my head and I didn't care. I was not being paid to know who shot John or who was pregnant.

During that time it seemed like that on a daily basis, my manager called me in her office with accusations of mistakes that other employees were turning in on me. It seemed as if they were trying to prove that I was not doing a good job. One day one of my coworkers got so tired of the ladies in the department who were always judging me and my work that she went off on a group of them in the break room and stood up for me! I was told that she scolded them about how negative they were and admonished them to help me instead of complaining about my work. We need more people like Shirley to fight for and achieve a positive work environment.

Eventually, my boss got fed up with my co-workers' complaints about my work. It seemed as if every time someone found something that I did, or didn't do on the computer they would race into the office and report it. One day she called me in the office and said, "Marene, what is this? She showed me a mistake that I had made and she started threatening me with a demotion or termination if she kept getting those system mistakes from my co-workers. That really concerned me, so, I thought I'd better start paying attention to what was going on so I could try to save my job. For some reason, I could not believe that I was the only person making mistakes in the department. That was hard for me to believe, so I started my own little personal research into those allegations.

I got involved because I couldn't just sit back and allow them cause me to fail. After that, while processing my customers complaints and reviewing invoices on the system I started recognizing mistakes that other employees were also making. They caused me to go there but when I identified my coworker's mistakes I corrected them and then I made copies and started setting up files on each one of my coworkers. Eventually I found at least one mistake on everyone in the department. The difference in the way I handled my work was that I processed and corrected the invoices as opposed to jumping up running into my boss's office. I was keeping copies in a file at my desk and when the opportunity presented itself, I took those files of twenty four corrected invoices that I corrected on each one of my coworker's entries and showed them to my boss. My goal was to remain positive and calm while demonstrating to her the difference in a matured employee and someone who was creating havoc in the work area.

I was analytical in how I politely shared my report with her. That also demonstrated how I had developed my critical interpersonal skills and it proved that I was getting ready for upward mobility. It also showed her how I protected my co-workers mistakes which demonstrated loyalty. Then I kept a file for her reference only when applicable. This better impacted customer satisfaction, I explained. She was baffled! "Oh, My God," she said! "When and why did you do this great work, Marene?" she asked. Then, I softly said, "Well, I thought I would do this mostly out of curiosity. I couldn't believe that I was the only agent making mistakes in your department. Therefore, I took it upon myself to prove this to myself. Now, may I ask you a question?" "OKAY," she said. "How many times have I come in to your office and reported anybody's specific mistakes to you?" And, she answered, "Never!" I told her that I corrected their mistakes and proceeded working rather than wasting time complaining about what they had done. "Our department is about satisfying our customers," I said, "and I enjoy my work and this has been an eye opener for me also."

Needless to say, that observation brought my boss closer to me and established respect between the two of us. She expressed to me that she had gained more respect for me because of the mature way in which I had handled that situation. I certainly learned to respect her for listening to my concerns. That served as another learning experience for me. **It's best to remain diplomatic at work and do your job and allow time and perseverance to prove who you are. Marene, 101.**

I couldn't forget what my life was like prior to obtaining that job. I also remembered that just a few days aforementioned, I didn't even know how I was going to provide meals for my family. Although there were still many challenges, we were progressing beautifully. I was learning how to survive and stay in the running in life. Sometimes when the weight of life caused me to become down and out I could always reflect on the past and make a quick attitude adjustment. I knew that nobody owed me anything in life. It was my own responsibility to survive and create my own "survival kit" for myself for and for my family.

I had goals and aspirations and would not allow anything or anybody to get me off track. I had to be the best employee that FedEx had ever encountered. The awards, accolades and commendations were often and plentiful. I was constantly being promoted and given special assignments because I could be trusted to do a good job. I maintained my perfect attendance status for a total of nine years before I took a sick day off from work. The first day I missed work, was when I had contracted a severe case of pneumonia. Not only was I faithful to work, I was also faithful to my husband, family and my church. **Faithfulness is a choice and it is achievable! Marene, 101.** One of the things that I learned early on in life is that I am in charge of my own image. I am also responsible for establishing my own reputation. Perception is the key. People could only read what I showed them. Thus, I soared in my craft of customer service. Later on, I compiled a notebook of my accomplishments. That played a major role in helping me to showcase my skills and talents whenever I was given a chance to promote up to a leadership position in the company. **You can't afford to leave yourself to chance, you must manage your present as well as your future. What happens to you in life is not up to other people, that wand has been placed in your own hand. Marene 101**

Little did I know that, my great attitude would play such an enormous role in establishing my future success! I was certainly headed in the right direction. **When you are trying to succeed and climb the ladder to success, keep in mind that adversity will remain your constant companion. I believe that adversity has a room in the home of success. Nothing comes easy in life. You are going to have to continually work hard, think hard and believe hard. Marene, 101.**

I could not imagine at that time, how my work ethic would also facilitate my life's purpose and calling. As time progressed, I found out that the company had established a new process for employees who were interested in aspiring to a management position. I pursued the L.E.A.P. Process which was an acronym for (Leadership, Evaluation and Assessment Process). I was very excited about growing into management and I really believed that I could achieve that goal. I was the first person in my department to apply for that opportunity. Then, I sought for the path that I needed to take to make in order to make my new dream come true!

One day, when I acknowledged to one of my coworkers that I was interested management she replied in a very cynical manner, "Girl please, you?" "You will never be a manager at this company." Then, she fell out laughing at the idea and I laughed right along with her because I believed just as strongly that I could and would become a manager. She thought that my idea was funny and that my aspirations were set too high. I thought to myself, who said that I needed her approval to believe in myself? I believed that all things were possible when a person believed, and by that time, I had already believed my way through many accomplishments. Therefore, I joined her laughing session and I probably beat her laughing. I was coming from a very different perspective knowing inwardly that it was only what I believed that determined my outcome.

I could hear that small voice inside me agreeing with my assessment of myself. Then, I asked myself, Why not me? I am as qualified as anyone else to become a management trainee. Oh yes, I can be a manager and I will! I proceeded and strived to accomplish my goal. My co-worker planted a seed of determination in my spirit when she laughed at me. That was all I needed to provoke me to contend against her disbelief. I went after management at breakneck speed! Once I applied for the management process, I immediately enrolled in a management theory class after work that the company was paying for. **Life is constantly charting a path for us as we float towards our purposes. Marene, 101.**

The first night of class was very different and exciting! I noticed that the professor had a unique way of getting the class to open up to her. She told the students to write down three things to introduce ourselves. 1. "Who we were and where we had been," 2. "Where were we going;" and, 3. "How would we know when we had arrived?" I had a story because I couldn't dismiss the fact that I had started my career under such extenuating circumstances and I was humbled by the road that I had taken to get there. I could see myself constantly making baby steps.

When I was given a chance to speak I stated that, (1) I was Marene and I had been nowhere doing insignificant jobs until I decided to return to school and improve my circumstances, (2) I was on my way to a management position at Federal Express, and (3) I would know that I had arrived when I become the president of a company. I would know that I had arrived when I could set one foot on top of my grave while the other foot is still on top of the ground and I could not find anything else to accomplish in my life.

Our instructor Kathleen laughed and told me to see her right after class. When I went to see her and we chatted for a few minutes, I told her how I had started the L.E.A.P. process and needed a little guidance. She then offered to mentor me and coach me into management. A few days later, I started going to her home one day a week for my special training. She volunteered her time and efforts to coach and train me as if I was taking a private class. That experience was another lesson in life for me and Kathleen's training was also an angel experience. There were times when we frustrated each other and sometimes we ended up screaming at each other. Many times I tried to give up but she wouldn't allow me to get off that easy. She was serious with me and she taught me how to think outside the box and stretch my mind to the max. She worked right along with me until her training had delivered me into a management position. Kathleen was a God sent angel who surrounded me and helped me to stay the course and to find my path to success. We are friends until this day!

I continued working on my regular job everyday, taking one and two day classes almost weekly. I was also still caring for my ill husband, not to mention that I was also continually playing the role of a working mother. By then, my oldest daughter was a young adult attending college and had great creative writing skills. I tapped into her skill-set and encouraged her to sharpen those skills while helping her mom to read and write my management business plan. We both stayed up together many nights working on my L.E.A.P Process paperwork. That was also serving to sharpen her communication skills. We were in a win, win situation. I had many assignments to complete before I could go to my panel interview. That process took me at least one year.

Good thoughts germinated my spirit as I went every where I could and did every thing I should to achieve my goals. All that mattered to me at the time was that, I BELIEVED! There was no stopping me. I believed that as I worked towards what I wanted to achieve that I would someday realize all my goals. I was driven and determined!

There were times that my husband became very concerned that I was trying to do too much. And, he would try to slow me down by laughing at me and making comments like, "Aha, girl, I don't know what makes "you" think them people are going to hire you in a management position at that company." I don't see anything that's wrong with that job you already got. Some people just try to do too much." Then, my reply was, "Yes me. Why not me? And, who are you to judge me anyway?" Apparently, I was wearing good blinders because I saw myself as having the ability to achieve anything I wanted to and I looked forward to proving him and everyone else wrong who doubted me and my capabilities. I kept my blinders on and stayed focused on my goals. I transformed my inner thoughts to use any discouragement that I received as fertilizer to grow my dreams.

Farmers use cow manure to fertilize their crops. Manure is food that's been processed through the cow's body systems and then deposited as waste. Farmers somehow discovered chemical deposits in that waste that activates growth. My personal fertilizer is made up of the manure of wasteful doubts, fears, and the disbeliefs of others. They chew on their doubts and fears all day and process it through their bodies and deposit it on to others dreams like manure. Inadvertently, I plant my seeds of achievements and when someone brings me their manure I use their negative chemical and lay it on top of my soil of faith and allow it to activate my career growth. When I lay doubts and fears on top of my optimistic attitude it trigger's growth for my dream. Your fear and doubt creates a stimulant that causes me to grow. Go ahead and plant your positive seeds for success for yourself. Pessimists create a subtle negative energy that once mixed with positive energies an atmosphere of growth is activated. That is because **positive energy is like a light and when light meets darkness, negative energy dissipates. "Light overshadows darkness." Marene, 101.**

Fearful people are afraid to live life which drives their dreams far out of the reach of faith. The lack of faith can cause someone to develop an internal system for the "Field of Pain." Marene, 101.

Remember that dream that I had where all those women were crying about their pain? The pain was caused by various situations in their lives that they did not learn how to process. They were hurting. **Problems don't go away they must be processed and processed properly. Marene, 101. As long as you sit there and grip an attitude of doubt, you will only be able to glare thorough your barriers of disbelief and miss your own calling and purpose.** There is a reason for everything under the sun. **Fear is a negative energy and it is also a wasteful resource when you are trying to succeed. Marene, 101. Positive people love a challenge! They enjoy winning and they will work hard while you are sleeping to prove to themselves and others that they absolutely can and will achieve their goals. Marene, 101.**

This is the kind of thinking that festers inside my spirit. Sometimes I do feel down but not for long because I realize that there is a solution to every problem. **I remained outside the box in my thinking because I had to leave room for innovation and creativity while solving life's situations. Marene's way!** I was surrounded by every obstacle that could cause me to fail yet I was succeeding. I could actually DREAM! And, I did. I kept the faith and I kept striving to achieve my goals.

Little petals of encouragement from the universe often dropped in my path in life. Periodically, something positive showed up and continually helped trod me towards reaching my destination. One example was, one day while I was leaving the Billing Service Center from work, running towards my car in the rain. I was thinking about how badly I needed a little money to help me to make it until payday. As I briskly ran across the parking lot with my head down blocking the rain from my face I noticed something on the ground that looked like money. Naturally, I checked a little closer and it was a twenty dollar bill. I couldn't believe what I was experiencing. I do believe in angels and I believe in miracles! Being in the right place at the right time is an understatement.

Things were not all bad. There were times when things were going pretty well for me and I was working diligently on my vision and plan for management. I was feeling very proud over all my good progress and my manager was in my corner. She was also coaching me and helping me all she could through the process. Finally, I knew that things were going my way, or, at least that's what I thought at the time. My manager was also constantly availing me with opportunities that were serving to develop my leadership skills such as; leaving me in charge of the department in her absence. By then I had been promoted to Team Leader in the Billing Center. She often delegated leadership authority to me, even when she was present in the department and that also gave me rapport with my co-workers. They had started looking up to me and I was doing great at that time! I felt a great sense of achievement!

Then, the bottom fell out of my little world. My boss assured me that she had submitted her recommendation for me to become a manager. That was absolutely required as a part of the L.E.A.P. process. The interview panel was going to be made up of members of upper management who would determine if a person was eligible to apply for a management position. Their decision was going to be based on several factors, one of which was the immediate manager's endorsement of the applicant. You must know that I felt pretty confident when I had completed all my assignments and turned in my paperwork. My manager assured me that she was going to recommend me and that I had her full support. On the contrary something else turned out to be the case. She was lying to me.

I had been through a one year preparation process for that great moment and now something else was taking place. Within a few days after my panel interview, I received a rejection letter from the L.E.A.P. Panel. Denied was stamped right at the top of the letter. I was devastated! What part of that process had I failed? I asked myself. Then, the bottom line of the form letter said, "If you would like feed back on our decision, please feel free to contact the chair of the panel (senior manager) Mary Mack and set up a feed back session with her. "Wow!" I thought there is hope and I got all excited again! I set up an interview with Mary so I could find out what I could do better next time. To my surprise I found out that my boss had not endorsed me to apply for management after all.

As a matter of fact, while at my feedback session with Mary Mack, it was confirmed in writing that my boss had instead wrote down in four places on her write up, why she would not be able to endorse me in her recommendation letter. Mary Mack said, "Marene, we couldn't have endorsed you even if you had walked on water." In dismay, I replied, "Why?" I couldn't believe what I was hearing. How could she talk to me like that? I asked myself. Then Mary responded, "Your manager did not endorse you, Marene." "Oh, yes she did," I said. "My boss personally told me that she had endorsed me to become a manager." Then, she stated again, "Marene you can review your paperwork and you will see that your boss never endorsed you." After I read the material that my boss actually submitted to the panel I felt such disappointment and embarrassment! My manager had allowed me to read a document, then, she had switched documents and submitted something different to the panel. She was a great pretender! Now, that's what I call on the job high level politics!

I immediately broke down and cried right in front of the senior manager in her office. How could she do this to me? I thought. However, immediately my determination stood up in me and suddenly I thought, I am not going to let her win! She was certainly not going to define me! I had to recover, and I did. **People can only do to you what you allow them to do. When you stay focused on your goals you will learn to take your obstacles with a grain of salt. Marene, 101.**

I made a quick mental and attitude adjustment. Yes, I was broken, but I was not destroyed. That was going to be another life's lesson that I could later use in my work. Sometimes people give up when they find out that other people have a hidden agenda and could care less if they succeed. I used that lesson to become better in office politics. I hadn't seen anything yet. That experience opened the door for me to handle many more political experiences in corporate games. That was going to be my new beginning. I had to wake up because it was nobody else's responsibility to take care of me in the corporate office, that was my role and I had to learn to watch my back. My mama wasn't there.

The letter stated that I had been given six months to return to the panel and the next time I was going to pass my interview. I was going to bounce back and, yes I was still aspiring to become a manager. Thanks to that fresh new lesson in corporate politics on the management level. Those office politics can get real nasty. I proceeded to learn the rules of the game so I could use my positive bat when I needed to knock them out of my field. And I did!

After I gathered myself, I asked the Chairperson if my manager could come in to our meeting that morning. Initially, she was a little apprehensive because at that moment she wasn't sure if it was appropriate. I assured her that I would remain diplomatic and professional. I wanted closure and I wanted to get an understanding of how we could possibly process through this matter. She then proceeded to summon my manager to the meeting room.

When my boss walked in and saw me in Mary's office, she immediately started to explain. "But, Marene," she said. "You were just not management material and I hated to tell you that." Then, I replied softly, "Sherri, why! You assured me that you were endorsing me. I believed you and now, you wait until I fail and tell me what you really think about me." I was so very disappointed! "Well, thanks for everything and I just wanted to let you know in the presence of upper management that I plan on resubmitting my application to repeat the LEAP process." I was already aware that there was a six months waiting period before I could return to the panel for an interview. Then I said, "I still believe in myself. I still believe that I will find a way to succeed and become a manager." After I left the meeting she was pacing close behind me trying to explain, but I never responded to her. I never did acknowledge her assessment of me. I learned how to access my own capabilities even in the face of difficulty. I had to rise above her opinion of me, and I did!

When we got back to the department everybody perceived that something was wrong and she didn't hesitate to tell the work groups what had happened. You can only imagine how fast her negative assessment on me spread throughout the department. Of course, she wouldn't take responsibility and admit how she had let me down. Instead, she laughed and told them that I was very upset because she had to admit to me that I really was not management material. She simply told them that I was angry because she couldn't see me as a manager. It didn't take long for the word to spread over the whole floor after she denounced me. Later, whenever I walked down the hallway, people sometimes giggled, jeered and whispered. Some people even told me to my face the fact that I was a failure and that if they were me they would give up on that venture. However, they were not me and I was not going give up on anything that I believed in! Some people stated that they felt that working in management was out of my league. And, my simple reply was, "I will die trying." I still had the last say over what I did in my career and their opinion of me didn't matter, it was just that, an opinion. I continued to forge full speed ahead adamantly persevering to fulfill my goal of becoming a manager at Federal Express.

A few months later, my boss was moved to another division in the company and a new manager was assigned to my area. Fate would have it that the replacement manager was also one of my former managers who already knew me and my work ethic. I already had rapport with Shelly, because I had previously worked for her in another department. Shelly didn't know like I knew, that she had been returned to my area for a spiritual reason. My faith was prone to work for me and help me to fulfill my purpose. **You never know why some things happen until you proceed to your next step and then it all comes together.** Marene, 101. Then you will say, AH, so that's why I had to experience that pain early on in my career. I didn't have to prove anything to Shelly. I had already proven myself when I had worked for her in the past. That was a new puzzle piece. Shelly didn't waste any time listening to my concerns.

During Shelly's first one on one session with me, I apprised her of my previous experience with my past manager. Of course, I also acknowledged to her that my confidence in management had now been somewhat tainted. Then, she promised me that she would work hard to restore my faith in management. She also assured me that my prior experience was isolated and that she would prove to me that she could turn that thing around. **Trust is a valuable tool so guard it at all cost. Marene, 101.**

As time progressed and after Shelly became acclimated to the work area, she made it a point to spend quality time with me and assess my situation. We had many sessions in her office and finally she pursued the L.E.A.P. process with me. When the time was right she recommended me to the panel again for a leadership interview. She was very honest with me and was kind enough to allow me to read her endorsement of me prior to submitting it to the panel. Next, she gave me the envelope and allowed me to hand deliver it to the proper department.

I passed my second L.E.A.P panel interview with flying colors! Two days later, I was approved by the panel to apply for my first management position at the company. At that point, my confidence level rose through the ceiling and I didn't waste any time applying for a management position. Two weeks after my endorsement and, after my second interview for a management position, I was granted an offer letter for my first new management position. I accepted the position, Operations Manager in Hub Operations. That signified one of the greatest accomplishments in my life, and I was ecstatic! Yes, it can be done!

One of my best friends and co-worker Gina was the very first person that I told about my good news! When she learned that I had been offered a management position, we both started hitting each other and giggling just like two little girls! Gina's cubicle was positioned right next to mine in the Billing Service Center. We had bonded sharing lunches, birthdays, baby stories, family events and work experiences. She had been one of my greatest supporters and cheerleaders in the department. Gina was always bragging on me and encouraging me. She was aware of my struggles and successes. She was always encouraging me and telling me to "ignore those fools." Gina was like the sunshine in my work life! She had a great positive attitude and she was full of fun! Now she was also there to celebrate my new secret with me!

I had just received a call from the hiring senior manager on that Monday following my Friday's interview. He wanted to offer me the management position that I had applied for. I was ecstatic when Tommy Jones said, "Marene, I want to offer you a position as Operations Manager in Hub Operations." He also told me to come to the Hub and sign my offer letter at 3:p.m. that same day. Of course, I accepted the position. After I hung up the phone, I was floored with excitement! I wanted to share my exciting news with someone because my immediate manager had not yet arrived at work that morning. Therefore, I immediately went to the next cubicle and crawled under Gina's desk. I was not going to share such important and exciting information with anyone else before my boss came in. Gina looked at me as if she thought that I had lost it. When she hung up the phone with her customer she joined me under her desk. After I told her my good news, we had our a private two girl's celebration under her desk! She was so happy for me! I had shut the mouths of all my critics at least for a minute. IT CAN BE DONE, IF YOU BELIEVE!

After my boss came in I went into his office, closed the door and closed his blinds. He was looking at me like, What? Next I told him my good news. The hiring senior manager had asked me not to announce my new position to the department because someone else from my department had applied for the position and he had not yet received his rejection letter.

My boss gave me a proud but surprised look and said, "Get out there right now and tell everybody!" I reluctantly went on and did what he told me to do. He was behind me pushing me and saying "Tell them," Tell them." People were getting off the phones saying, "Tell us what? I gave in and told them that I had been offered a management position in the Hub. After my announcement everybody in the department was standing up and amazed. They were shocked because hardly anybody knew that I was applying for a position. Lots of people were asking questions and praising me. I had been very private in sharing my information in the past because Sometimes being negative hinders a person.

Chapter 10

Some of My Lessons as an Operation's Manager

Wow! I was finally an Operations Manager in Hub Operations at Federal Express. I was overjoyed because, again I had beaten the odds that were stacked against me! It is something about winning that keeps me playing the game again and again! There is a spirit of joy that comes with winning and the feeling that flows through my veins can not be duplicated. My wildest dream had come true! I was about to encounter a major change in income which could afford my family to experience a much better lifestyle.

My first night as a new manager in Hub Operations was very exhilarating. Many of my former coworkers warned me not to wear my church dresses, suits and high heel shoes to the hub. But, "Marene" had a mind of her own and went right on out there and wore those high heels and a business dress. I was walking around on tour with Mary Tom, who was an existing manager assigned to familiarize me to the culture at the hub.

The first thing I noticed was that we had to walk on a catwalk which was positioned over the heads of the hourly employees. Those guys were having fun looking straight under my dress. The funny thing was that I couldn't do anything about it. Early on in the night I became miserable. I never imagined that we would be on our feet all night and soon my feet started streaming in pain from wearing the high heel shoes. We covered lots of territory on our feet while walking on concrete all night long, whew!

The funniest thing happened at the end of the night. We were about to return to the office area and by then my feet were killing me. "Them babies felt like they were broken." I had walked all night in those high heel shoes. I was so ready to sit down. Finally we were headed back to the office area. I was very exhausted! Mary Tom was walking and I was tipping.

Suddenly she said, "Let's go out there and see the MD 11." I didn't have a clue as to what that meant or what the significance of the MD11 was, but I agreed to go with her. Where else was I going? I didn't know my way around anyway. Then she said, "Let's catch this people mover." Things were happening so fast and I was thoroughly confused. We are out on the ramp, it's late somewhere near dawn, my feet and the rest of my body are crying for relaxation and about two hundred planes were lined up roaring while being prepared to launch. I was craving to stop, quit, or do nothing and now another tour to see the MD11, Oh my God!

Then, Mary Tom flagged down a people mover and when it stopped she stepped up on to the people mover and sat down. Since that was new to me I followed suit, but something happened. When I attempted to step up on the people mover, it took off and all I could do was hold on to the rail and run to try to keep up. When the people mover got out on the open ramp, it picked up speed and all I could do was to hold on and run faster to keep from being dragged to death. The next thing I knew I was running so fast behind that people mover that I could actually feel my heels kicking me in the booty. Needless to say, nobody could hear me hollering because every thing and everybody were all looking forward and I was in the back. Not to mention that my voice was competing with all those roaring airplanes out there on the ramp. Nobody could hear me anyway, so I had to let my will to survive take over my thoughts and RUN!

Oh Lord, I thought, they are going to kill me. I opted to stop streaming and grip the bars for life. Nobody could hear me anyway and I needed all my breath to run. Finally, Mary Tom looked around and said "Oh God, stop this darn thing." The word finally got up to the driver and he stopped the people mover. I fell flat on my face and didn't have enough breath left in me to speak. They all thought that I was seriously injured. I just wanted to get some wind back into my lungs just enough to tell all of them to get out of my face. When they discovered that I was okay everybody thought that they would die laughing! Needless to say, we finally arrived at the ramp to tour the MD11 but I was still in a daze over my dragging experience. Had it not been for that dramatic experience, I probably would've been a little more enthused while touring the MD11.

My high heel shoes were torn up and left on the ramp and I cannot describe the Condition of the business dress that I was wearing. Take a lesson from this and listen, when someone else has already been there, Marene. I am glad that the lesson was not about picking up a deadly snake.

My first work group as a manager was another experience to be reckoned with. As I sat in my first management meeting being introduced to the other existing managers, I was puzzled by the fact that nobody wanted to manage a certain work group because of their reputation. Although, I was a new manager I felt the urge to volunteer to manage that group. I insisted on managing them even against the insistence of my senior manager. He had insisted to me that I lacked the management experience necessary to handle such a challenge. However, out of curiosity and my dare devil personality, I was having difficulty understanding what could possibly be so wrong with the work group, so I took the challenge.

The existing manager whom I was replacing failed to notify the group that I would be their new manager until the last minute. That decision played a major role in projecting a cold reception for me when he introduced me to the group. Needless to say, my first night with the group was a little turbulent. Later, I set up one on one session's with each one of my employees. After that, I was able to identify and correct all the discrepancies. I then took time and worked through all their issues one by one. Next, I implemented corrective actions. Soon I had turned the group around.

Eventually, they became motivated about working for the company. For example an employee had't received her paycheck for several weeks because the previous manager had issued her a mis-sorted check and had failed to correct that mistake. I stayed at work overtime and went to the proper department and got that corrected and appealed to the company to reimburse the employee for her bounced checks. That action started to create a loyalty for me amongst my work group. Productivity improved in my area and soon we went from forty five (45) percent to eighty-five (85) percent productivity in just a few months. That correction along with a few other improvements changed the morale in the work group. That year my new work group threw me a surprise birthday party. **All people need is to be valued and treated with respect. That's common sense. Marene, 101**

I was able to transpose my innovative and motivational skills to my management position and promote productivity in my workgroups as a manager and eventually I was again out performing many of my peer managers. My reputation started shinning in the area of management. My performance reviews started to become excellent and I was growing in my new position. I was always getting accolades, awards and recognitions. I eventually became one of the top performers in the management ranks at the Hub.

I believe that innovation is the key to positive and powerful change and it can be used to propel you through any walk of life. No matter what you do and where you go in life, never lose track of your common sense. Marene, 101

A little later in my career, I was assigned to work for a different senior manager, Catherine Slaxe. I immediately admired her because she had made it to the level of senior management. She was the worlds best at provoking her management team to think outside the box on the leadership level. For example, she was always deliberately setting up scenarios where we were required to think in order to find resolutions to difficult situations.

Catherine actually set up make shift mind-change sessions. I will never forget the time she showed us a special training video where, "Five adults ended up traveling together on a hot summer evening, on a dusty road without air conditioning, windows down and dust flying through the windows dirtying their business suits on their way to Abilene, TX. All of them were extremely upset because each one of them reluctantly submitted to taking that trip while thinking that they were pleasing the other person. Their failure to communicate caused each one of them to think that the other person wanted them to go. However, everybody ended up unhappy and upset because nobody really wanted to take the trip. Isn't that how it is sometimes in life? How many times have you done something that you never wanted to do but you did anyway because you thought that you were pleasing someone else?

That is indicative of most people. Some people have a tendency to follow the crowd even in work related situations and everyone involved end up unhappy giving giving each other the eye. The morale of that story is, think for yourself and make your own conscientious decisions that result in your own happiness. **A person will never find his own authenticity if he allows his surroundings to dictate the directions that he takes towards his own life's destination. Marene, 101.**

Catherine's leadership often validated how I already felt. She often took out time and held private training sessions for her managers in her office after work and I remind you that we were getting off at 5:00 am. Working for Catherine changed my mind-set and set me on the path towards becoming an accomplished leader!

A few years later, I was assigned to work for Randy Brooks. By then, I had become a seasoned manager. I had more than ten years experience under my belt. After I had experienced so many successes, one night I encountered an incident that threatened my whole career. And to think, with that particular incident, I actually created a self-inflicted problem. My leadership skills were challenged when I failed to follow through on a mandate from my boss.

Randy Brooks mandated that all his managers ensure that all hourly employees were in compliance with Ramp Safety Training. In an effort to assist us he designated one manager to do the training and the rest of us were assigned to send a few people to take the Ramp Training before the sort every night. His goal was that we be in compliance by that Friday night. That was simple enough. However, I failed to prioritize all that week and in my procrastination I tried to cram all my people in the training within a couple nights. By that Friday night I had too many people left to train. My failure to follow through on my boss's plan rendered poor results such as, having to send most of my group to training before work on a Friday night. That's bad management. I was out of compliance in more ways than one. Friday nights were the most critical night of the week, not to mention that, my boss was out on vacation that week.

Although, I asked my employees to please report to work immediately after the training, needless to say, the opposite occurred. My group trickled in to my work area at their own pace without a sense of urgency. That wasn't good for a Friday night sort. Due to an equipment breakdown Training already had lasted longer than planned. Things seemed to be falling apart for me that night. Since we started out behind the eight ball, consequently, we caused a thirty minute late sort down. That set off a chain reaction and we grounded thirteen (13) flights which resulted in a major lost for the company. I WAS IN TROUBLE!

At the end of the sort I had to face my boss Randy Brooks who had to be called back in to work from off his vacation. He was mad enough to kill me. I had been one of his best managers and had always had stellar performance. "Not you Marene" he said. He was stunned! I was asked to explain to him how and why my area had failed. I was scared to death and devastated because I had never been disciplined before. I was more accustomed to awards and commendations. My feelings were really hurting and my heart was skipping beats. In fear I had conferred with one of my peer managers who tried to help me to make up a good lie to tell my boss. After lie rehearsal I went in to see Randy prepared to clear myself with a lie. However, fear of the unknown made it difficult for me to remember the order of my lie. I really desired to blame someone else for my mistake. Surely I hadn't made such a foolish mistake, not "Marene the great!" However, when I saw the look on my boss's face I had a hard time remembering the specifics of the lie that I contemplated telling him.

Randy confronted me again while using some very sharp choice words and said, "Marene, tell me how you managed to drop the ball tonight!" Something within my spirit insisted that I be honest and tell the truth and accept responsibility for my actions. Suddenly, I banned that lie and told Randy the truth. "I took the risk and procrastinated." I said, "I put off my training until the last minute and it caught up with me. I did not do my job and I accept responsibility for my actions." Then he said, "I had planned to fire you tonight Marene, but since you told me the truth, I am going to give you a warning letter." "I am very impressed with your integrity." I accepted my letter like a woman because it was my leadership failure. That letter remained on my file for eighteen months and I had to suck it up.

When I got home the next morning (I was still working on the overnight shift) I was very sad and emotional because I had caused my own trouble that time. When I told my husband what had happened he fussed at me and told me it should've happened and I should've been more attentive to my work. I felt terrible over his response and cried even harder.

The next day I called my brother in Chicago and told him what I had done and how bad I felt. He had senior management experience and after he consoled me he advised me to develop an Action Plan. I had never written one before and he and his wife (who was also a professional) walked me through the process. The plan consisted of all of the area managers teaming up and sending people to critical areas versus sitting around waiting on an area to fail so that they could point their fingers. My plan was about the big picture. Using my recommendation would prevent one person from causing everyone else to fail because ultimately, all of us had failed together. That action plan was basically fail proof. It was about how everyone working together would prevent failure. My idea was, to take failure out of the hands of one person and to extend success into the hands of everyone. The bottom line was profit for the company.

When I returned to work that Monday night, I presented my plan to my boss and he was so impressed that he took me to the Senior Manager's meeting and they allowed me to present my plan at the meeting. That plan was implemented and was used throughout the area to improve overall performance. Eventually, I received accolades for the Plan that I created. **Innovation is the key to powerful positive change. Even some of our worse experiences can create life lessons that can help you to define who you really are. Marene, 101**

A few years later, I founded a community service organization called, Choice, Inc. Although I was still working in management at FedEx, I started feeling a void in my life. I felt a calling upon my life to do more. I knew that I could do more and I was not being fulfilled in my life at that time. I had accomplished so much with just a little, and I became passionate about giving something back to the community. I began to desire and find ways to train other women, who were still out there in that "Field of Pain." I wanted to show them how to take charge of their lives just like I had done.

Eventually, I formed a community service organization six years prior to retiring from FedEx. I named the organization Choice, Inc. because I knew that everybody had a choice in life and that they could also make better choices on a daily basis.

By then, all my daughters were grown my husband was stable. It was time for a new chapter in my life. I faced many more challenges and successes in my hub management position. However, I had learned more from experience on how to navigate through my life and through my work experience.

Once I conceived the idea, I got busy developing my idea into a business structure. There I was again, working through the challenges of starting a new non profit business.

I had accomplished a certain level of success in my management career. I believe that everything that happens under the sun for a specific purpose. I never lost my spiritual mind-set or my faith. I had already done lots of volunteer work in the community over the years through Fedex and through other venues. I also recognized that many women were still out there and I had learned lots of life lessons and had had many experiences that would help other struggling women. Consequently, I wanted to offer my assistance back into the community and to help others.

I started that my business, Choice, Inc. in 1996 on a whim. I was still working at Federal Express at that time and my husband was also still sick. Yet, felt the calling and the desire to do something else.

I set out to build Choice, Inc. with my own hands while developing and implementing my own ideas. My goal was to design skills training classes that would empower, train and develop women in the area of Mindset Change and Motivation. I wanted to offer, Computer Training, G.E.D. Preparation, Professional Imaging and Job Placement Assistance.

I developed a very effective board of directors that helped with the planning and implementation of that program in the community. I will discuss a little more about Choice, Inc. later in this book.

Chapter 11

The Birth of a New Dream and My Vision

irthing a dream can become as painful as a mother's delivery pains. The process can also become as strenuous as labor and delivery. There is no way to have a successful delivery without following the proper process. You can attempt to circumvent the process and do it your way but it could cause the process to become longer and more painful. **Once a mother conceives a child, she can count on the birthing process to take place at the predestined time possibly about nine months later. Marene, 101.**

Arbitrarily, once your dream is conceived it also enters into its predestined birthing process. Your purpose and calling become activated and it is growing inside your spiritual womb. Then while waiting for the appointed time, you can nurture your own authentication. You have a birthright and have been born with certain talents and gifts and you can start looking into your own calling and finding a way to develop your own gifts. You are preparing to deliver a God given talent into this world. Your talent was placed inside you at conception and now your time has come to take the steps into your place in society, in your season. God stamped you with a seal of authentication at birth and you are who you are because of it. You have an identity and you can not change yourself. Nobody can be you except "YOU." Develop yourself and prepare to take off. This is about your dream, your calling and your purpose. You have it but you must use it, ONLY YOU can do this!

Many people have refused to step in to their rightful places in life so they have pain. Some dreams have been distorted by procrastination. Then, they waste precious time dealing with a multitude of issues in life and end up just feeling pain. Please don't abort your baby (your dreams talent, purpose and calling). You are destined to make your mark on this great society. Keep on pushing because pushing is the only way to get the baby's head down into the birth canal and ultimately give birth to your child (your dream).

Once the baby's head comes out you have done the hardest job but your work has just begun. Let the body of the baby flow naturally. Although it may be painful, it is all a part of a major process. You can only be guided by the flow of the process. There are rules and if you work against the rules of birthing, you may abort your baby (dream). I am talking from my own experiences of giving birth, both to children and then to my dreams. The greatest joy comes after the baby is born! Sometimes, it may seem like the birthing process is killing you, but hang in there, you will not die. Birthing is a very difficult process. Feel the joy that comes after the baby is born!

Becoming successful is just as difficult. If you were born for a specific reason, conceive your dream and get pregnant with the development and birthing process. Take your eyes off other peoples dreams. Just like you can not birth someone else's baby, you also cannot give birth to someone else's dream. Their purpose and their calling is theirs! You can stand by and wipe sweat from their brow but they have to birth their own dream. You can only birth your own child or dream. If something is growing inside you, it is your baby, dream!

There is no easy way out so, take that word "easy" out of your vocabulary. You may fool yourself or other people but God will only be pleased if you develop the talent he placed in YOU at birth. You can only prosper from your own calling. Your purpose was developed in God's master plan and it is needed as a part of the society in which you dwell. You have something to offer and if you hide or abort it you will be held accountable for that because you are defying a plan that God created and planted inside of you.

Chapter 12

My eyes have seen the light!

$\mathcal{I}$ started seeing real purpose in everything and I could also see how purpose was propelling me towards my own destiny. I knew that I had accomplished many goals and that I could someday share my experiences with others and incite them to also succeed. I deliberately kept a good attitude as I went through many difficult times. I knew that some of the things that were happening to me were for my own good and my development. From a spiritual perspective, I also knew that life was teaching me those valuable lessons so that they would sustain me until the appointed time for my manifestation. I knew that someday I could "C E L E B R A T E" my life's lessons because of all the good that had been planted inside me at birth. I also knew how my work would impact this society. **I was born to teach and my "Life" is the teacher. I am a seed and it all is derived from my "LIFE's lessons and experiences. Marene, 101.**

Now let's go back to the street revival that I dreamed about in the beginning of this book. When you have an opportunity to help someone, help them! The street is the central station. We all interact in the streets of life. The street represents what's public and general. Everybody is out there in the streets of life and everyone has a right to the streets. Nobody has the power to stop anyone else from being in the streets. The streets belong to everybody and anybody; therefore, we are all out there in the streets of life.

I started understanding to the meaning of my dreams. Those people who were lying out in that open "Field of Pain" were the people who were perpetually hurting over the cares and snares of life. There wasn't any place for them to eliminate their pain. No worldly systems had been set up to manage all that pain. Everybody in this present life is hurting from something and they are crying inside about something or somebody. The "Field of Pain" is synonymous to a land field. The pain was derived from the cycles of life and ended up in the land "Field of Pain." Once you are out there you can't help yourself and you don't have a clue as to what you need to do or what to expect. It is just lots of old baggage and life matter.

All that pain is derived from life's set-backs, disappointments, failures, regrets, delusions, doubts, fears, jealousy, denial, regret, hate, pride, rage, drugs, crime, death, toxic relationships, divorce, bitterness, despair, desperation, false religion, waste, poverty, racism and the list of disparities goes on.

All that pain has festered, rotted and evolved into perpetual hurt. That pain has lain there for years and the machines of life are stampeding over it, crushing it up and moving it around but not eliminating it. So the pain just lies out there in the "Field of Pain" and continues the hurting. It is a carry over because it was not delineated in the proper places in life. That pain has been recycled from one phase of life into the next phase of life and it has become perpetual pain. Sometimes people don't even have a clue as to what's happening to them. There is enough hurt to go around. Some people have given up and they lie out there in the "Field of Pain" crying, moaning, groaning and pleading for someone to help them. At this point in the process they are willing to receive help from anyone who is willing to share in the resolution of their pain.

While I was living under the gun of despair, I chose not to allow life to engulf and devastate me. I realized that I had too much to learn and even more to offer the world. I knew that I had a calling on my life and a purpose for being born. If you have surrendered to your life's purpose and are working in your calling you are either a part of the pain or a part of the healing process. I also knew that many people would cross paths with me and we could share in healing each other's life's pains. However, one must be willing to acknowledge that his pain exist before he can accept his healing.

That "Field of Pain" is out there holding people who can't seem to find their way back to their life's path. That's what my dream was about. It was about the people who had lost their way in life. They started life with a clean slate. Their pain was caused by issues such as, bad relationships, alcohol, drugs, false religion, fake Christianity, low self esteem, unresolved anger from past hurts, cluttered lives, unresolved issues, other people's clutter, problems that seemed too difficult to solve, abuse, hate, rape, stresses, frustration, low education, no education, crime, deceit, and etc. Some people had experienced disappointments until they had given up and resorted to the "Field of Pain." Others had trust issues and failures that had mounted and grown out of control. There were many reasons that the women were lying out in the junk yard of life waiting for someone to help them and to put them back together again.

I finally learned how to chart my life according to my purpose and navigate my way to fulfill of my own destiny. The only way that I could do this work was for me to get involved in my own calling in life. I am obligated to use my life where ever I am in the universe. All the events that have happened in my life were charting my path and propelling me to my destiny. Now that I have birthed my calling, I can grow and develop into my destination while I am on this planet.

Sometimes when I look back at myself as a sixteen year old high school dropout, devastated and lost, it never occurred to me that God had allowed me to have that experience to put me on the path to learn lessons that I would eventually have the opportunity to share with the rest of the world. Although I came to Memphis to finish high school, I had no idea that I was just beginning a new journey to my destiny. I was being placed on a track to be slated right into the slot in life for my calling.

That plight eventually led me to homelessness. Although my parents were still living, they were in Missouri and I was in Memphis. When I first came to Memphis I moved in with my paternal grandfather. However, I was only able to stay with papa for one week. We had our differences and I knew that I had better leave while I was ahead. A distant cousin picked me up and I moved in with him and his wife and family. I stayed with them until a few months before my graduation. He was an alcoholic and things got so difficult that I decided to remove myself from that situation. A few months prior to my graduation I moved in with a girlfriend and her husband. By then I was working and going to school and I thought that everything was going well. However, one Saturday after I returned home from work I found all my belongings stacked at the door. I was devastated! I had only one month left before graduation. My friend had packed my belongings and set them at the door so I would understand that I was being evicted.

I didn't have a clue as to why she had put me out. I was homeless and didn't know what to do about it. I was only nineteen years old with minimal survivor skills. I didn't know where to go or who to turn to. I was determined not to return to Caruthersville a failure. Therefore, I decided to walk over to one of my closest classmate's house and told her what had happened. I was crying copiously. After we discussed the situation together in our little way, I went back to the duplex and sat down on the front porch and continued crying. In about an hour a car pulled up in the drive way. It was my friend and her big sister, Bernice. I was sitting on the front porch next to my luggage crying my eyes out. Her sister then sister got out the car and started loading my luggage in her car. Next, she came over to me and said, "Come on," I got up and followed her to her car. By night fall I was settled in her home and she made me very welcome. I knew then that she was an angel sent from God. "I was hungry and you fed me, I was naked and you clothed me; I was homeless and you sheltered me. Bernice (rest her soul) didn't have a clue that she was fulfilling God's plan for my life.

Two days after I graduated from high school, I married Curtis Austin. In a few days Curtis & I drove to Caruthersville and picked up my daughter whom I had left in the care of my parents. They agreed to take care of my baby until I had finished high school. Mama, daddy and my sister had taken good care of my child for two years and now it was time for me to take care of her myself. They were determined that I was going to get my education. I had great parents and a strong supportive family! They gave me a second chance and did everything that they could to help me to move on in my life. I was born to the right parents at the right time. My sister also stayed home after her graduation and helped my parents with my baby. She delayed her career after her graduation because she also wanted to support me until I was back on my feet.

One of the greatest pains that exist in the world is "Regret" because once you make a choice and your choice seems to be the wrong choice, you are likely to regret it for the rest of your life. Ultimately, you can end up in the "Field of Pain" hurting forever. Now the antidote for regret is to "Let It Go." It doesn't matter if it's your fault or not; LET IT GO! The best thing you can do for yourself is to let it go! Forgive yourself, forgive your offender, forgive your past, AND DON'T LOOK BACK! As I reflect on that "Field of Pain" that I initially dreamed about, I could see the pain of regret all over the place. I wish, I could a, I should a, I would a! That is a deep sore and it carries constant pain. LET IT GO! That is the only healing balm for such pain.

Life has tracked your destiny so tap into your resources. Sometimes certain events in life are destined to drive you towards your path to success. They are created by the universe just for you. Then, when a curve ball is thrown it will set the tone for your future.

There is a purpose for everything under the sun. You have just weathered a bad storm and you really desire to reach your destination safely. However, the wind is too high for you to continue in your present direction. You can find a way to maneuver around the wind and find another way to get to your destination. Sometimes life creates a deliberate detour for your growth. That's just like the wind of a storm blowing you in a different direction. Years later the sun will come out and the storm has passed over then you will understand why you had that experience. **Life, proliferates Life! Marene, 101.**

Life is not all bad. Sometimes it seems as if people primarily have the propensity to accentuate the negative. I venture to contend that that there are a higher percentage of good people than we can imagine.

Chapter 13

Absent Dad's

May I reiterate, all Black men are not necessarily absent from their families. All black men don't necessarily leave their homes and abandon their women and children. I had a very strong father who was present in our home and in our lives. He took the lead as the head of our house and treated mama with respect. Society has a tendency to portray most black men as absentee fathers. No! I can raise my hand and say that my daddy was present in our home. He often proclaimed that "these are not Uncle Sam's Babies. These are my babies and I will take care of my own children," and he did. Whatever it took, he supported his family. My daddy stepped up and took responsibility for his home. No, we didn't always have all the essentials, but we had enough love among ourselves to make up the difference.

We were raised with lots dignity and pride! If daddy had to go across town and shovel snow in the winter when there was no work he did just that. He made enough money to feed his family every day. Sometimes he made just enough money to buy sugar, flour, and a little piece of salt pork. I think it was called fat back and streak of lean salt meat. When he came home he and mama worked together making that into a meal. Sometimes, we had syrup, fried fat back, a whole cake of bread, and a large glass of cold water and went to bed. We were all full.

Daddy was totally in charge and available all our lives. We never heard statements like absent fathers in the home. My daddy was a devout Christian disciplinarian who made sure we went to (1) church, (and may I add, on time for every service) (2) went to school, (again, present and on time everyday), and He also made sure we studied and learned and we reported to him what we learned at the end of every day. He helped us with our homework and we'd better pass our classes. He also attended the P.T.A. meetings. He was absolutely going to show up wearing his big wide brim brown hat while holding mama's hand and she too was wearing her big church hat. We always felt embarrassed because daddy was so outspoken and we never knew what was coming out of his mouth. Daddy stood up for what believed in and lived by his own opinion. And, (3) we were going to work. Daddy's main philosophy was that "If a man doesn't work he ought not to eat." He was a Bible fanatic! I believe he knew every chapter, verse and word in that whole Bible.

I hated that darn Monday night Bible study and prayer that daddy led in our home; especially after I became a teenager. We all knew his rules about being on time for the 9:00 a.m. Sunday school and we were always running because our feet were our transportation. Daddy would already be at church standing by the door checking his watch to ensure that we were on time, or else, God, have mercy on us! That was also without regards to the weather.

There were no government food stamps back then. We were lucky if we managed to get the commodities that were issued once a month. Most people were poor and needed the supplemental government cheese. Most families consisted of eight, ten and twelve children. Therefore, it was a blessing to bring home that government cheese. Sorry, I just had a nostalgia moment!

Daddy had lots of sayings that we all lived by: "These ain't Uncle Sam's children so he won't have to feed mine. We are going to work for what we get. You have a mind, that's your own "personal possession." Daddy advocated that, "If you work for what you get, it's yours." "Make sure you save, "Put something back for yourself, pay God, pay yourself and pay your bills." "Don't let anybody put your hands in the fire and get the goody out." "Your bounds are set and you can't go over them." "Don't let no man hit you girl, if he hits you once, he'll hit you again." "Look girl, you can always come back home." "All grown people should have their own house." "There's going to only be two grown people living in this house and that's me and yo mama." "At about fourteen years of age, you should be deciding what you're going to be doing when you get eighteen, because you will be leaving this house." "You'd better be going to college, getting a job, going to the military or starting your own business or something because you're going to be leaving here when you get grown." "Now, don't be sitting there looking at me like a Saturday Night Koon." "Now straighten yourself up and fly right." My daddy, (bless his heart and may he rest in peace) was always joking, using clichés and reading that Bible. He was quite a character. "Are you looking at your mama funny? You know, she could've pushed in on that little soft spot in the top of your head when you were a baby." You're going to respect your mama and your sisters boy!, Yay hear?" I can't forget that one about, "don't let anybody put your hand in the fire and get the goody out."

He taught us how to show respect and he demonstrated respect especially for mama. No! He demanded respect for mama and if you lost it and failed to respect mama, you were in some kind of danger. That not only applied to immediate family, it also applied to everyone else that came in contact with his wife. Daddy walked his talk and he taught lessons with his life. He said what he meant and he meant what he said.

Chapter 14

Preparation for our Life's Work

*L*ook at us now, we are the baby boomers that built America and have constantly made history in our own communities. We are the educators, business owners, doctors, lawyers, clergymen, mayors, talk show hosts, actors, community leaders and life changers of today. We expect our children to turn out the same way we did nevertheless, we did not raise our children the same way we were raised. Maybe it will help if we refer to some of our roots for guidance.

As I reminisce over my progress, sometimes I got so busy that I felt a little apprehensive about sharing everything that I was doing with family and friends for fear of criticism. People were always cautioning me, praying for me, and telling me to slow down and take my time, but unfortunately they were not along with me when the bills were due. Okay, as much as I respected and appreciated their prayers and good advice, I felt compelled to do what it took for us to make it in life. I believe that it takes different things for different people. My rainbow was not the same color as their rainbows.

For example, one Saturday evening back in the day I was sitting on my bed arranging my lingerie feeling very troubled over our situation. Curtis was lying on the couch relaxing and the children were all on the floor playing. He was getting extremely sick at that time and we didn't have any idea of what was going on with him. I was sitting there shedding tears.

My phone rang and my friend Caren, who lived in St. Louis, was on the other end of the line and she said to me, "Marene, why are you sitting there crying like that?" Astonished, I replied, "Girl, where are you?" Then I peeped out the bedroom window. How did she know that I was crying? "I am in St. Louis," she said. "St. Louis?" I said, "Then how do you know what I am doing in Memphis?" She got spiritual on me and said, "He just told me to tell you to pray, I am going to let you go." By then, I was broken into a thousand pieces. My emotions got the best of me. Could this be true? Is God actually watching me like that? Then, I fell on my knees, right there at my bedside and prayed. "Help me Lord!" Ha, Ha, Ha!

Suddenly, out of nowhere, my inner voice spoke to me and said, Get up right now, Curtis is not going to die. Curtis is healed! Without thinking or trying to make sense of that situation, I immediately got up and ran into the living room, grabbed Curtis by his arm and said, Curtis you can get up. God said that you're healed! Then, he looked at me and said, "You'd better leave me alone girl." I knew that look so I stepped back and got out of his face. At that time he was very sick and he was in constant pain.

I was excited and happy because I believed what I had heard in my spirit and I continued rejoicing. That was hope for me and the family. I started shouting in a praise dance and my little children joined in. I had experienced a sign that we would be okay. That good news brought me joy! So I told my oldest daughter to get on that piano and she started playing shouting music for us. All my other daughters and I started dancing and rejoicing over daddy's healing. And I held on to that faith. Curtis just laid there and ignored all that. But that didn't affect how I felt or reacted.

The next day, I went to church and testified about what had transpired at my house that Saturday night. Then, I started shouting again and running over the church floor. I was not ashamed or shy about what I believed in. That time the church people joined in and rejoiced with me.

I believed what I heard in my spirit with all my heart. Little did I know that this would be the beginning of a real hard test of my faith which would actually guide me through out the rest of my life and my career.

It is amazing how life plays out on a platform of experiences and lessons. About three days after that episode of shouting, Curtis relapsed and we had to transport him back to the hospital. He was admitted and placed in Intensive Care. Then, everything that had just happened started to seem like an optical illusion or mirage. However, I kept the faith! Although the evidence of failure was inevitable, I stood up for what I believed and would not lose my faith. The prognosis did not support my faith and the diagnosis actually contradicted my faith. I would not let go or give up! I disregarded what I saw and heard from the doctors while I remained true to what I believed in. I absolutely wouldn't take it back!

I stayed close to my girlfriend Aretha who was always standing by to boost up my faith and she believed right along with me and constantly urged me not to let go or to give up. The doctors encouraged me to give up because according to what they saw, he would not make it in his condition.

I did not flinch or waiver. I felt that if the Bible was right and it said that "God could not lie," then the doctors were in error. I really believed that God has spoken those words to me and I started to resolve within myself that God made him so he knew more about him than the doctors anyway.

Later, a conference with his doctors confirmed that he definitely would not make it. They told me to give him up because he could not live very long in that condition. That information went right out the side window of my head. I refused to believe anything negative. I asked them what was their prognosis, and I was told, that if he lived fifteen more days that it would be a miracle. Then I said, "Well, look for a miracle, because God told me that he was going to live.

Needless to say, soon after that Curtis got up again and eventually he went back to work and worked for several years before he became very sick again.

That same type of activity went on for the next nineteen years and we went back and forth. Although he was not always able to work and most of the time I took care of him and the kids, he was not an absent father. He was faithful in whatever he could be faithful in. He took his family to church every Sunday, helped the girls with homework, cooked when he felt like it, and he was a good house husband. **Something positive can be extracted from every situation whether it's good or bad. Marene, 101.**

I had been blessed to make many accomplishments while taking care of my family. Life has presented me with many rich experiences. Not only had I accomplished much, I had achieved success with few resources. One day I started to reminisce, hmm, how could I package my testimony. How can I share these life lessons and experiences and benefit other people?

I reflected back on those dreams once again as they had left an indelible impression on my mind. That inner voice has always been there with me giving guidance. In my dream there had been thousands of hurting women in that open field that I have named, the "Field of Pain." When something becomes confined to a field there is an indication that it has become widespread.

Everybody is hurting over something. I am connected with their pain because I have experienced so much pain myself. That was my point of connection to the hurting women. I remembered all that crying and tugging at the women and trying to heal their pain with what I had in my hand. Now I could identify more with the pain because I had also learned how to appropriate my own pain. Tuck it away or not, one must deal with it at some point in life.

Complaining and worrying doesn't comfort you when you are hurting. Something soothing needs to be applied to the pain and a little compassion will surely bring relief. If you can find the root cause of the pain then there can be a healing from the inside out. By now, life had served me a ton of blows and I had learned how to box in that ring of life's arena.

To this day, some people haven't learned survival and coping skills. Many never learned how to fight life back, so they fall down, lie out there and cry over the pain of disappointment. That method is not the solution to the pain. That concept has compelled me to remain close to my roots and in the streets and share my story with other hurting people. My idea of the streets here is representative of, "where the people are." My dream was not just about women, it was also about all people. The women represented reproduction. Most people are harboring hurts from past incidents that have happened to them in life, reproducing more and more pain.

As I ventured into my life's work I found myself talking to anybody who would listen to me. Then, I would also gravitate to anybody who would show any sign of interest in the views that I was portraying in my conversations. I was going to get to where ever my destination was taking me. I was feeling inspired because I was making progress. At that time, although I could not give it a name, "a new baby was growing inside my spiritual womb." It was another little girl whose name would someday be called "Choice, Inc." That was the beginning of the higher calling which had been placed on my life and my perspective forever!

I wanted to follow up and fulfill my three nights of dreams. Then a brainchild idea came to me and it would add another level of purpose and direction that my life had taken.

I had been on the processing table for years being prepared to do my life's work. I had learned that even if life served up unfavorable experiences there were reasons for those experiences and the outcome would become life lessons. I had also learned that my response to my experiences could influence different outcomes. As certain events occurred in my life, I had a special way of observing an experience and listening while seeking for the lesson that the experience was destined to teach me. That concept induced my desire to transmit this same message to others. They could also learn how to view the positive implications from their own experiences as they looked at them from the rearview mirrors of their lives and succeed against the odds, the same way I had learned to reflect.

By that time in my life I felt compelled to fulfill the calling that was on my life. Finally, it had become very clear to me what I was called to do at that point in my life. At the onset I knew that I was feeling led to start reaching out to help other women who I knew were struggling with life without the sufficient skills that they needed in order to take care of their families. I had just graduated from that same level in my own life. I also recognized that God had brought me this far and that he would take me further as I ventured towards my calling and destination. I remained obedient to my inner voice as my gift was plugged in to the universe. I also believed that if I could dream something, I could also achieve it.

As I went on with my life as usual I sometimes felt a little indignant and impatient because things were not happening fast enough for me. I guess I was always waiting on that great "lighting bolt" experience! But things were just not happening that way. Things were not happening for me in a cut and dry cookie cutter process. That would've been too easy and I would've missed out on the real lesson.

Then, just at the nick of time when nothing special was on my mind, a strange chain of threatening events set off in my life. Little did I know that I would encounter such personal catastrophic experiences! The first thing that happened to me was that, I noticed one day that I was having a serious shortness of breath. I didn't have any idea where or when that started. I also noticed that I was experiencing a sudden weight loss. When I went to see my doctor I was diagnosed with pneumonia. After intensive treatment and a one week hospital stay, I returned to work and went on with life as usual. However, I started paying more attention to my health.

A year later while I was still dealing with life and working at my Hub management job, I was stricken again. That time, while driving home from work one morning, I felt a sharp chest pain. I had just pulled a fourteen hour shift and I thought that the pain was from the stress and strain. However, as I continued towards home, I felt another chest pain. Immediately I went into denial. I couldn't be having chest pains, I am just very tired and I will get plenty rest this weekend, I thought. I am going to do better about my body, I promised myself. I was very tired and exhausted because my schedule seemed to be none stop. However, my plan wasn't panning out because there was something very different about those particular pains. They persisted and became more severe. I decided, well, maybe I will just drive myself on out to the emergency room.

When the doctor checked me out he said, "Marene, your blood pressure is 177/ 157." They immediately admitted me and placed nitroglycerin under my tongue. Then a few hours later, my Neurologist gave me admission instructions.

"Marene Austin, you've had a stroke!" "No!" I replied, "I don't have time for no stroke!" "I can't afford to be down sick like that!" "This must be a mistake, Dr. You probably have the wrong chart!" "Are you Marene J. Austin?" "Yes sir," I replied. "Then, I have assigned you to be admitted to the hospital so we can treat you for a stroke." "But, I have a family who needs me and I need to take care of them," I begged. "My husband has a muscle disease and he cannot work, so I can't be having a stroke!" The doctor just looked at me in dismay and said, very calmly, "Mrs. Austin, you have been assigned to room number 723." I couldn't believe that this was happening to me. I felt like everybody needed me and I was having a stroke. "Oh My God, what will happen to my family? They all need me.

My mama, sister, two of my brothers and their wives came to Memphis from up north to see about me. After a week's stay in the hospital, I was back at work. I had a stroke that had not left me with any physical evidence. That was another miracle! I knew that someone bigger than life was taking care of me and within a few weeks, I returned to work and to life as usual. I knew that I was suppose to be doing something spiritual with my life but could not for the life of me figure out what I was supposed to be doing. And my excuse was; how I was going to do something and did not know what it was? None of that was making good sense to my rational mind and that was not easy. I would not get involved and try to follow a vision at that time. I needed a cookie cutter to make the vision more clearly to me.

I often heard my inner voice saying that God had something special for me to do. Sometimes I felt empty because I was still out of my place in my life, but I just wasn't getting it. Then I started to think, am I delaying my own vision and purpose? Why can't I stop! I somewhat continued to allow "the issues of life" to drown out my spiritual thoughts. The more I did it, the more I did it.

About a year later while I was still working at my overnight management job, I felt a strong stinging sensation in my rectum. That was extremely unusual! It felt like squirrels were playing around in me back there. I had had a chronic case of hemorrhoids for over twenty years but that time it was different. After I tried the usual over the counter medications to no avail, I went on and scheduled my doctor's appointment. After my examination my doctor explained to me why surgery was going to be the only solution to my problem. That was indeed the worse thing that's ever happened to me! When I recovered I was in excruciating pain. Due to complications, I ended up spending another week in the hospital then when I was released the pain persisted for weeks. Time off from work was predicted for two weeks and I ended up being off from work for a total of five weeks. That severe pain persisted the whole five weeks. I almost worked my poor little mama to death with that ordeal. Even my ill husband often tried to help me find relief.

Late one Saturday evening while I was lying in bed, quietly crying and feeling sorry for myself because this time things were not going right. I started praying and asking God, "What is it? I thought that maybe if I would get all spiritual and make a few more promises to God that he would stop me from hurting. All I knew was that this time my pain was different and persistent. I started to reflect back over my whole life. So many strange things had happened along the way. Now, is this my calling to ministry? I thought. What about the women in that "Field of Pain." That experience of pain that I was feeling was certainly softening me and quieting my big mouth. I started projecting more humility in to my thought process. That spiritual test had started to wear on my mind and my attitude had softened.

I wanted to get well and return to life. I was accustomed to being in charge and now I had to submit myself to the mercy of others. I went internal and appealed to my emotional side. I asked my inner voice to please help me to think through that maze. I wanted to please get up and to stop the physical hurting. I also wanted to find some balance in my life and be okay. At that point, I decided that maybe I was off course in identifying my calling and finding my ordained direction. So I committed to looking in to what it would take for me to run that "Street Revival," that I had dreamed about a few years ago. By then, I was willing to run out in the streets until my calling found me if that method would help to bring me some relief.

I was ready to do something even if I had to break something! Somehow I knew right then that I had been broken and that I was molded and shaped for my calling. I no longer was going to resist the calling that was placed upon my life. Neither was I ever going to be lackadaisical about God's work again! I made a pledge to God and to myself.

The work that I had been called to do was about that forgotten generation. It was about all those hurting people who were lying out there in that open "Field of Pain" that I dreamed about. I remembered how they were all lying out in that open field moaning in pain, because no body had been assigned to reach them. There I was jumping over some and touching others trying to help. They were on my account and they were waiting for me to get involved in my work. Oh, my God! I had the solution! I was holding a scroll in my hand. It was the vision which had been placed in my hand in that dream. I remembered that I was holding on to it very tightly. God had trusted me with an anointed talent that he had placed inside me for his use. I had to use it! That was what I was holding onto in that "Scroll." THE MESSAGE WAS ON THE SCROLL WAS MY STORY! Wow! Now I get it!

The hurting people in that "Field of Pain" had been counted out in life because they had been given no voice. And I had been given the awesome task of giving voice to their pain. My God given motivation and inspiration would serve to heal!

They were hurting because nobody would "C e l e b r a t e" them for their true worth. Rather than being valued, these people were stereotyped and considered counted out in life. Those people were hurting because society had given up on them for one reason or another. Sometimes society would even go as far as to say, that they "didn't want anything out of life."

They had been judged everywhere they went by everybody they encountered. Life had dealt them fatal blows and it was up to them to survive. Some of them were inducted into "life" at an early age and sometimes under unusual circumstances. That fact had caused them to fall prey to their own misfortunes. Now other people in society did not believe in them which sometimes caused them to lack confidence and to also not believe in themselves. They lacked the knowledge, skills and resources to fulfill their own dreams and purposes and ultimately had fallen into a state of oblivion in that "Field of Pain."

I also observed as I desired to reach out to help them that these were everyday people. They were ordinary people that God had created, and they were destined to become "extraordinary." They had not yet learned how to decipher the greatness out of their own lives. They did not know that they could believe in themselves. They had been judged severely and incorrectly by others around them. They were capable of doing great things in life and some were even qualified to do exploit's. However, they had been told too many times that they had nothing to offer society. In the meantime, life had beaten up on them so many times that it had left them hurting, bleeding, hollering and crying in pain. Constant failures and set-backs in life had caused them to give up on themselves.

These people were some of the most talented people on the face of the earth and they could create marvelous things. They were creative and innovative and they were strategic improvisers who knew how to make life happen for themselves and for others. However, they did not recognize their own talents because they were being exploited by those "POVERTY PIMPS." They had never been exposed to the knowledge that they were actually born with the capacity to use their own talents. They didn't even know that their talents had been extended to them by God. Those hidden talents that they possessed had meticulously been placed inside them at birth. That talent was plugged in as a part of their frame work and make up.

They were wired at birth to do great things! My assignment was to use the "Scroll" to help them to reconnect their original wires so that they too could succeed! The lack of knowledge was causing these people some great pain! Yes, they were hurting!

In the meantime, those "SOCIETY POVERTY PIMPS" were banking on their ignorance and hoping that they would never wake up and realize that they had gifts in their own rights. They all had birth rights and did not know how to develop them. I had been given all this information on the "Scroll" that I was holding on to while running behind that Black Stallion in my dream. I was assigned to share this information with other hurting people so that they too could learn, then they would also become successful. There was a "Scroll" for them in life and it could also be placed in their hands.

They were hurting because they had never been "C E L E B R A T E D!" for their resourcefulness and they did not yet realize their true worth.

Peace of mind is a treasure that lots of people never get to enjoy in their lives. Marene, 101.

Some of this pain was caused by the obstacles in life that had forced some of these people to abort their own "Vision Babies." Some had dropped out of high school and college. Some had even chosen wrong careers because the fear of the unknown had caused them to abandon their dreams. They had settled for worthlessness and dread. They panicked over the pain of not being able to complete things. They lacked motivation and inspiration in their lives, so they virtually settled for the "mediocre." Some were hurting just from complacency. Some of these hurting people had been sidetracked by the ploys of individuals who had promised to love them but had dropped them in mid-air. They pledged to never love again because they were still hurting over unresolved relationships. They had lost their ability to trust love again. The innocence of love was a thing of the past. They had given up on the very reason that they had been created. They would never find the strength to navigate their own lives back to normalcy. They were all experiencing the "Pain of Regret."

In the heat of the moment many had conceived children and passed down curses to the next generation which gave rise to generational curses. That had caused some people to not even have the ability to identify inherited pain. That was unending pain and they were without an exit plan. Those hurting people had never realized that they had been created for Greatness! Some of their pain was self-inflicted and had caused life disruptions.

Imagine a fish being out of his water, flopping on the dirt shore outside the lake. Look at him and see how miserable he is as he tries hard and harder to get back into his water. Now if that fish gets back into his elements he will live a long time and survive. However, if he cannot get back in his water he will indeed die in the wrong place. That's exactly how it is when people are operating outside of their talent, purpose and calling. They have found themselves out of the elements that God has designed for them to reside in. Their purposes and calling is the only place in their lives where they can survive, thrive and become complete, happy and fulfilled.

If a person has been wired to be one thing and he is trying be something else, his life will become calamitous! That hurts! A natural born talent has been ordained just for you and nobody else can do what you were born to do. If you have abandoned your talent there is no way that you can get off your treadmill to nowhere.

One time, I decided to drive up to Missouri to pick up my mama for an evening event at my home in Memphis. Everything started out beautifully! I had made that trip many times before. When I got to Caruthersville, mama and I left C,ville in plenty time to arrive back in Memphis on time. However, fate gave us a different spin. On our way back we noticed that the exit sign read; Detour Take Outer Road to Memphis. We exited on to Outer Road, no problem.

While driving and chatting I finally noticed that Otter Road was taking us in the opposite direction from Memphis. Outer Road was taking us somewhere else. When I asked mama "What must we do?" She replied, "I don't know." Then, I stared in my rearview mirror and noticed that an eighteen wheeler was right behind me so I stopped and flagged him down. To my surprise, he said, "I don't know ma'am, I am following you." Oh Lord, I thought, the blind is leading the blind. There we were, out in the middle of nowhere without direction. I thought for sure that a truck driver would be more knowledgeable about directions than I was and he is looking to me for direction. We were lost indeed, and nobody knew how we could find our way back.

As I continued driving, I noticed a house out there in the middle of no where and that there was a little old man working outside in his garden. I pulled over and asked him how I could get back to the expressway that led to Memphis and of course he told me. Again, when I turned to head back to my car the eighteen wheel driver was still trailing behind me. Sometimes people depend on you even when they know that you don't know where you are going. We did arrive back in Memphis on time for my event and we laughed at that experience. **Sometimes the unexpected will happen in life, but it's what you do about it that matters. Marene, 101.**

If I had not noticed that I was going in the wrong direction, that story would've turned out a whole lot differently. When I recognized that I was on the wrong track, I surmounted that obstacle and sought directions to get back on the main drag. The farther you travel in the wrong direction, the farther you get from your destination. You may get there but it may take you much longer than planned. I probably wouldn't have been able to pull off my event. **Life teaches us lessons as we go. Life can absolutely serve up some unexpected challenges but we can't afford to allow them to distract us from reaching our destination. If we stop we can end up in pain because we are out of our places. Marene, 101.**

Those hurting people that I saw in my dream were the people who go to work everyday but they are treading on a perpetual treadmill to no where. They work for food without a clue as to where they will end up in life. Many have never set goals so how will they know when they reach their goals? If you don't know where you are going, how will you know when you get there? They are getting no where because they can not see purpose in their rear view mirrors of life. What does real success look like anyway? Is it money? Does it look like material possessions? Is it big houses, flashy cars, vacations, jewelry, boats, money, expensive vacations, prominent and affluent friends, acceptance? Can you measure the signs of success?

Many people are working hard to make someone else successful while they settle for mere crumbs in life. Some even allow other people to determine their success. They seem to be "trapped in the jaws of a viper" and they feel that they can never discover or even visualize their own purposes. It takes everything they can do to make it from day to day. Maybe they would feel better if they could search within their own hearts and spirits and find their true life's purposes and calling.

Life consists of more than merely food, shelter and clothing. We can have it all in life. Think about what brings you the most joy. What are you very passionate about? What would you rather be doing than anything else in the world? **What makes you want to play your inside music?** Some people wake up every morning regretting to face another day at a job that brings them no joy. The only thing that makes them happy is clocking out in the evening. They capitalize mostly on creating havoc in the lives of others because that is the only way that they can feel power. **It equates to a sickness when one's happiness is powered by invoking pain on others. Marene, 101.** They are hurting so badly that they go to bed every night and hurt themselves to sleep.

Many people are afraid of venture because of their fear of failure. They dare themselves to dream. Dreams seem to be way too far to out of reach for them. The cares of life have cluttered their dreams and clouded their visions like a cataract over a person's eyes. Their vision is blurred.

Those hurting people were crying over the lateness of the hour in their lives. By then life had served up lots of reality and they were left lone, by themselves with no place to turn. They were being mentally used and abused by those system bullies, those "Poverty Pimps" who are very skilled in mind manipulation. Those hurting people are everyday people, people just like you and me, people who had serious talents and potential but hadn't quite learned how to make that talent work in a way that it would serve their purposes. They lacked the knowledge and the much needed resources that it would take for them to phase into mainstream society and maneuver towards their desired goals and their full potential.

They had no power and nobody would "C E L E B R A T E" them for their true worth. These people were in constant pain because they had tried to be accepted and were constantly rejected and made to feel like they were nobody. In the meantime, their talents were stolen and used by the system bullies who lacked talents themselves but wanted to appear as, "The talented!" Those talented people who had so much to offer the world had been manipulated by the worlds system bullies that they were actually afraid to own up to their God given talents. Those money grubbing bullies were always around like poisonous snakes waiting for another talent to be created so they could kill someone's dreams or at least strike them down.

The funny thing about all this is that the system bullies could also be talented but they were hurting and bleeding themselves. They had to fight day and night to steal the talents of others in order to mask their own pain. They were the most fearful! They didn't believe in themselves either and was certainly not going to work for what they could take from the weak "talented" people. They wanted to get to the talented while their talent was in its infancy. They refused to process their own lives so they lie around and procrastinate so they could steal talent from others. They have never concentrated on themselves because they have spent their valuable time focusing on someone else.

Their fear was of the hard work and time it would take for them to develop their own talents. So they spent all their quality time stealing somebody else's talent. Their pain derived from crawling around looking for a way to catch other people off guard and then snatch someone else's authentic ideas. It never dawned on them that God could also put his anointing on them and they too could produce something great from within themselves. They just stayed busy waiting on someone else to manifest. Their greatest concern was that, "ITS MONEY IN THAT!" They actually spent their valuable time in life looking for and smelling for MONEY, just like the GIANT in the nursery rhyme, "Jack and the Beanstalk," who said, "I can smell the blood of an English man." They chanted, "I CAN SMELL THE TALENT OF A NEW MAN!

If life is offering you lessons and you allow those lessons to become invective you run the risk of constantly repeating lessons. Just like school kids who have to study to learn lessons and pass tests, experiences in life are lessons to learn. And growing from experiences is like passing tests. One must study his life material in order to succeed in his purpose and calling. Nevertheless, if you are perpetually failing you are holding yourself back in life. Then a downward spiral to disaster awaits the weak. You are destined to grow as you go so you can plug your talent into the service of the universe.

If your growth is warped you will be hindered from moving into the next phase in your life. Life can offer you the same lessons in different ways. These lessons can then become perpetual, lasting much longer than they were originally designed. Then, as you continue to reject learning, eventually those lessons can become continual curses. Once lessons lay inside your life stream and are not used for your growth, they can ultimately become routine and habit forming developing into incorrect lifestyles. Then they can hurt you more than help you. Later you will pass your pain on to others.

They felt trapped because they had grown old and yet they hadn't made any progress. That had become a main "Pain Center" for them. They go out and check themselves in to the "Field of Pain." There is nothing left to look forward to. Yes, they hurt, they cry like babies crying for mama's milk.

One of the greatest pains that exist is the pain of jealousy. Rather than finding their own purpose, some people risk using the sickness of jealousy to covet someone else's gift.

Once a person allows jealousy to enter into their system, they loose their ability to release their own creativity. Jealousy is a poison and negative energy that eats a person alive. The Bible defines a trait of jealousy as, "cruel as the grave." Thus, the grave has no feelings and it is cold. Once it has a hold on you, it won't let go. Nobody has a desire to face the grave and when it become imperative; the thought is to get it out of there quickly! Jealousy is a choice. A person can escape the jaws of jealousy by celebrating the successes of others as opposed to resorting to destructive methods.

Chapter 15

The Second Day Dream
about the Church

*T*he second day my dream focused on the church. Church was initially designed to become a place of refuge and strength. What happened to the preacher's concept of what God has designed for them to do? In my dream it seemed like preachers had deviated away from their calling and become caught up on money. They were called to preach the gospel and had resorted to preaching gossip. They looked thoroughly confused in my dream! Ultimately, they had passed their confusion down to the masses of people. Now the people had started worshiping preachers instead of worshiping God. Many preachers had become entertainers and MONEY GRUBBERS. They had taken advantage of the offerings. Instead of taking care of the widows and disadvantaged they had started prospering and taking care of themselves, their families and their special interest groups. They were exploiting the down trodden and weak minded. They had started running marketing strategies and various schemes in order to heap finances upon themselves. They would lose their visions of saving souls and they too had become "POVERTY PIMPS."

Their ultimate agenda's was to create a great life for themselves off the backs of the disadvantaged. They prospered from the unlearned and innocence of some of their followers. Rather than train, enlighten and empower people, they took advantage of people's lack of knowledge and resources. They would never value or celebrate "creative thinkers." They were threatened by independent thinkers unless they could influence their opinions on them and cause them to think like themselves. They prided themselves in keeping people in the dark even though they had lost the drive to take care of the widows and the disadvantaged.

They sometimes esteemed themselves higher than others and lifted themselves up. All of this reality was so overwhelming that some people had opted to remain maimed, blind and in denial. They had no concept of their own progress and didn't even know that success awaited them. They had locked their minds up in prison and some had thrown away the keys. They had given up on their dreams, their calling, their purposes and their visions. Success seemed too far away from them because their minds were on lockdown. They refused to think and allowed someone else to think for them.

They used the church to mask their pain. They pretended that they were genuine and practiced spirituality on Sundays and on special occasions. Some of them had genuine talents but lacked the wisdom needed to allow their true talents to surface and to be used as destined. Sometimes they operated from the opinions of others. They were far from reality and feared being judged or regimented by big religious systems.

That type of behavior had caused many preachers to fail and miss their own calling and purposes in life. Many of them were the great "Money Grubbers" who had found ways to pimp the weak and helpless in the name of the Lord. **I know that this is not exactly descriptive of all preachers nor of all churches, but, "If the shoe fits, wear it!" If it doesn't fit, leave it on the shelf so the real Cinderella can wear it. Marene, 101.**

Chapter 16

The Third Day Dream Interpreted

*I*n my third night dream, I was running behind a Black Stallion horse as fast as I could, while I was holding a Scroll in my hand.

That vision was designed to be used to heal minds through motivation. I had to protect my vision so I was holding on to it very tightly. Nobody would be able to take it away from me because I realized that it had been placed in my hand by a higher power. It was destined to be used to serve my purpose on this earth. At the end of that dream, a voice told me that I would run a revival. Oh, I know! I've got it. I am the "Wounded Healer." Healers run street revivals. If I am assigned to the streets, then to the streets I must go. That concept represented doing what I do outside the walls of the church. That is the ultimate of grassroots work! There are No strings attached and no one can dictate where I can serve, who I can serve or when I can serve, this work cannot be hindered. **A hungry child doesn't care where his food comes from.** Marene, 101.

People can be motivated to think freely and to think for themselves. Motivation can count as a bond payment to free minds and allow people to become free thinkers. They will no longer be ruled out of life by a lockdown system that actually has no power over their minds. If only they knew that it's all an illusion and that delusion is planted in the mind. They had chosen to keep their minds on lockdown. Some have rejected the keys that unlock their minds so they are hurting over not being able to realize their life's dreams and promises.

Something has to trigger the mind for people to believe in themselves. The system bullies are depending on them to remain maimed blind and Asleep and to never find mind freedom again. They have stolen your talents and ideas and are banking on your ignorance as collateral to regain control over your mind. Imagine how it must feel to produce a product that you have invented and someone else is enjoying the benefits?

Chapter 17

My Wide Awake Vision

vision was given to me one night and I got up and wrote it on the computer and saved it. "I AM PREGNANT."

I AM PREGNANT!

I am pregnant with a new idea
I am pregnant with new concepts
I am pregnant with a plan
I am pregnant with resources
I am pregnant with connections
I am pregnant with opportunities
I am pregnant with finances
I am pregnant with volunteers
I am pregnant with advisory members
I am pregnant with a staff
I am pregnant with buildings
I am pregnant with choice sites

On a daily basis, I can feel my baby moving inside my womb! Sometimes she kicks swirls, punches, turns-over and many times shivers as she awaits the day that she can be born.

The other day an ultrasound confirmed that she is a girl. This was determined by her reproductive system. She has the ability to develop, grow and even to give birth to other little Choice sites in other cities, states and even in other countries.

And, you my dear friends may share in the joy as the first to know! Now that you know, what are we going to do about it? You are the fathers, grand parents and even god parents of this great child.

You are expected to be caretakers and or find alternative care for this child. Your love for little Choice will demand you to ensure proper nourishment, training, growth and the love that she will need in order to be a productive part of our social-economic society.

So, what is my point as the mother who is carrying this great child? We have things to do places to go and people to meet.

This load is getting mighty heavy for me to continue to bear along. The weight of this child is slowing me down. I need you to come under the load. How? You may ask. Take my hand. I know where we are going. I have been to delivery many times before. I need you to become a more active part of our child's life.

No longer will you be allowed to sit outside the delivery room; watching television, drinking coffee and coke, talking on the phone and walking the floor while waiting on the announcement that we have delivered. Come inside with me. Hold my hand, wet my lips, give me a chip of ice, wipe the sweat from my brow, and watch, as our child comes forth from my womb.

We will experience the joy of delivery together! There is nothing like it! The time has now come for us to give birth to a new concept. It's called EMPOWERMENT, in every sense of the word. Never again will we sit and wait for a proposal to be granted. We have too much talent among ourselves. We will step outside the norm and set our own boundaries. We will get involved and create our own opportunities to succeed!

Our clients will now be called our customers who will later become our business partners.

We preach self-sufficiency; let's practice self-sufficiency!
We preach talent; so, let's show some talent!
We preach abilities, let's demonstrate some abilities!
We preach opportunities; so, let's go out and find some opportunities!
We preach business relationships; let's build some business relationships!
We preach achievements; let's achieve something!
We preach success; let's possess success!
We preach innovation; so, let's innovate and create!

Self-sufficiency; in every sense of the word! No longer will we sit and wait for someone to recognize that we exist. We will produce and reproduce and use our God given talent and make our lives count.

Put on your cap and gown and come into the delivery room with me. We are about to deliver! A new little girl is about to be born! But she will need to use your arms, legs and feet until she can stand up on her own two feet.

Then, she will deliver to me a voice. It will be a speaking production. MOTIVATION! That's how she will make her mark on this great society! Give me the hurt, give me the pain, and give me the sorrow. You only have it because you chose to hold on to it. Choose better for yourself! Success is rightfully yours, but you must take it by force! Believe in yourself and believe your God given ability to succeed.

You have untapped talent and resources. Go after it! It runs down like a flood and pours out of you like a pitcher of water. Only you can develop this talent. It is unique to you and for you and only you can create it. IT'S YOURS, IT'S YOURS, IT'S YOUR'S!

Chapter 18

And Her Name Is Choice

A few months passed and one night in November, 1996, while I was attending a family Thanksgiving dinner in Chicago, IL, I offered to make an announcement to my family. My time had finally come and mama quieted the crowd for me and set the tone for me to testify to my family. That night I felt like I was having my coming out party! I told more than seventy family members that I was starting a business. I HAD TO DO THIS!

There I was, standing in the middle of the floor before my best critics and I was speaking as if I had good sense and feeling very good about it. I had gone through a long process to get to there. That was one of the most exciting moments in my life! Finally, I was making my entry into the world of "my calling" unequivocally. All my family were taking me seriously this time and listening intently to what I had to say. There was something very somber about the spiritual mode in the house that night! Everyone was in awe over my announcement! After I was done talking, a few of my family members immediately started fielding questions like the news media. That process felt very good and special to me. I loved it!

At that time all I had to work with was an idea and faith in God. I was taking my first step of faith into the unknown world of business. I didn't have any idea how much I didn't know about starting my own business. However, when my family asked questions about my idea, I felt like I was being trained and prepared to learn. In actuality, arbitrarily I was also announcing this to myself. I just had to start somewhere. That was a very innocent and authentic moment for me. I had been given the mold and it was being poured from the life of Marene J. Austin and now I could use my life for good.

Chapter 19

Fulfilling the Work

When I returned to Memphis from Chicago, I knew what I had to do. I felt very serene about all the different events that were happening in my life at that time. It was time for me to take the steps to start my business and I was ready. I had just entered into a new dimension in my own life. I stood ready and willing to do whatever I was supposed to do with those hurting women. My inner voice became more prominent as it started guiding my every move. It seemed more like all my past experiences would now become useful and good lessons that could help others. I was very eager to get started on my work even though I didn't quite know exactly what I was going to be doing. I didn't waste any time getting started. I was under the influence of my voice and I started doing everything I was told to do.

Everything I did for the next few months was centered on fulfilling my vision. I believe that once a person enters into obedience to her life's work the inner spirit will be in agreement with her positive energy. Then she will be able to attract everything and everybody that God has created to help her to get His work done. That was all about Gods' divine plan for my life.

I had developed many skills through various work and life experiences and at that point, I was in a position to transpose those skills over and start my own business.

Everything happens for a reason and along that time I had started to realize that all my learning experiences could be used as I set out to prepare myself for this great work. The volumes of information that I had gained from various resources, as well as, all that I had served to shape my mind-set. I had developed great leadership skills, and I had also worked in various business capacities throughout my career which had enhanced my strong leadership skills.

Once I entered into my work of finding my calling, many individuals, coaches, clients, professionals and volunteers were attracted into my path. I received lots of encouragement and inspiration as I set out to develop Choice, Inc. It seemed like most of the first three years of my business development were spent receiving guidance, coaching and mentoring from various business consultants and professionals.

For example, one of my friends who was already an accomplished businessman and who had lots of Board of Directors experience reached out to help me and offered his guidance. He had served in my capacities in positions at various Fortune 500 companies. He was very astute in business acumen and he shared his knowledge and expertise with me as I sat out to start my own business. Alan has remained available to help me and he also volunteered as one of Choice, Inc.'s first board of director's members. Both Alan and his wife Rena have been my cheerleaders for many years throughout my business ventures and throughout my life.

I was also fortunate to tap into the expertise of a very special guy at United Way of the Mid-South who also personally set aside his time and advised and coached along as I was developing my business. He was concerned and offered much assistance in helping me to understand the strategies of not for profit business' establishments. Sam Jackson was also very instrumental in helping me to obtain business management training, office space, equipment, supplies and many other doors of opportunities as I worked to get my business off the ground. I was introduced to Sam by one of my daughters who also had experience working in the non profit business.

I will never forget meeting Bells Rickman who learned about the work that I was doing in Through the landlord at my office. At that time we had an urgent need for computers to be used in our computer lab. Bells Richmon, who was a very successful businessman, initially donated around thirty computers and soon became a very productive board member at Choice, Inc.

He also donated a personal lap top computer for my personal use. Later, he gave us an LCD projector. Again, on one unassuming day he and one of his business associates picked me up for lunch. To my surprise, they actually took me to Office Depot in Germantown and awarded me with a surprise office shopping spree! I was baffled! I was told that I could purchase anything that I needed at my office that day. Bells was laughing and said to me, "Marene, you can get anything that you want out of here." I needed so many things and hardly knew what to do. They both pulled out shopping baskets and were asking me, "Do you need some of this and some of that." The clerks at the store were also helping me to shop because I was spaced out.

When we arrived at the check out counter, they burst out in a loud laughter when I offered them my discount card. They were more interested in obtaining a tax-credit. That was indeed another miracle! It seemed as if my angels were unlimited as I continued to develop Choice, Inc. I always felt surrounded by a band of angels. I followed the directions of my inner voice every day as I continue doing on a daily basis until this day.

My business was growing and it was built solely on my own knowledge of my product. That product is, ME AND MY LIFE. I set out to impart myself and my knowledge to other hurting women who needed my help. I lived it, slept it, walked it, talked it, and toiled with it day and night until I developed it. It was all about how I was able to overcome and how I had surmounted the insurmountable circumstances in my own life. I continually leaned on my faith which was rooted in a greater power. I believed that the forces and influences from that greater power were going to continually open both spiritual and natural doors for me.

Choice, Inc.'s mission was to "empower financially challenged individuals to become self-sufficient and self-actualized by providing them with the necessary tools that they needed to create their own opportunities to succeed."

I had a story that was about the steps, perseverance, hard work, training, development, and prayer that it took for me to care for my family as I sought to succeed against the odds. I was constantly seeking to find the directions that I needed to create opportunities to fulfill my own vision.

My vision was about how God had allowed fate to inundate my life when I had no idea how things would work out. God combated for me and he gave me the strength to endure hardships and allowed those experiences to eventually become life lessons. It was all about how circumstances in my life had gotten out of control and how I had been vulnerable. When I cried out in despair, God protected me from devastation. It was about how I never gave up or resorted to lower energy thoughts that sometimes evaded my mind. I kept right on pushing and believing through some of the darkest times in my life. It was about how I learned to use my faith in God to help me as he also guided me through every test. Then he gave me a testimony at the end of each experience.

My story was built solely on the path which was leading my life through the universe to my calling. There were times when it was hard for me to visualize the trail that I was blazing. The reality of it is; once you have walked thorough a certain woods over and over in the same way enough times, eventually you can look back and see your tracks as they begin to blaze your trail. At first there isn't any sign of a path. However, if you keep walking, you will eventually blaze a trail and someone else can come along later, follow your steps and also reach their own destination. **You are blazing a trail with your own life. Your path will make it easier for another person who comes behind you and follow and also find their way in life. Marene, 101.**

I eventually became a model for other struggling women because I became a face for welfare moms. I allowed my voice to be used to give them a voice. I realized that I was talented, authentic, genuine and idealistic because one day I learned to recognize that God had bestowed all those talents on my life. Authentication was my birthright! Life lessons are only created to help a person to recognize who she is, where she is going and how she will know when she gets there. **You are not a copy, you are authentic. You can not be somebody else and nobody else can be you. You must face the naked truth and bask in who God has made you to be, because only you can be you. Marene, 101.**

I had to recognize that I am Marene. Only Marene can be Marene, that's the easiest thing going on in my life. I cannot be anybody else and nobody else can be me. I am an original design, made by the creator and there is none like me in all the earth and never will there be. I was predestined to be Marene and in my season I was destined to flourish as I acknowledge my calling, fulfill my purpose and leave a legacy for the next generation.

It seemed rather strange that my story was the key that opened doors for me to found my own business and also operate in the business that God had given me to do. When there were opportunities for me to meet with other business associates I almost always started every conversation sharing my story, which ultimately was the Choice story. People often expressed to me that they were inspired by my story. The testimony that I had acquired through my trials and tribulations was my signature. The obstacles in my life were charting a path for me to someday share my experiences with others and inspire them. That was due mostly in part to my positive attitude towards those experiences whether they were good or bad, I could always see how God was working in my favor.

My story was as much about a higher power as it was about my life. I was always testifying about how God made provisions for me and how He always remained with me. He comforted me and gave me peace and soundness of mind as I faced many catastrophic experiences. People often commented on my joy and cheerful spirit and how I handled situations through using perseverance. They were inspired when I told them how things worked out for me at the end of each one of my life's tests. I also always shared stories about the lessons that I learned along the way from each experience.

Instead of crying about what was happening to me I normally resorted to the inner thoughts of, what was I expected to learn from each experience and what did I need to do better the next time? I refused to succumb to lower energy thinking (i.e. I can't, it won't, I give up) and lose the value of the lessons to be learned. I made a sacrifice to do what I felt was right in every situation even if it was uncomfortable or dissatisfying. I am humbled as I share this information because I remain amazed over my life and how it is ultimately playing out.

I learned that while life offers many tears, fears, highs and lows, expectations and the unexpected, disappointments, failures and embarrassments; life is also full of joys, celebrations, happiness, laughter, successes, love and dances that all come together to make a person complete. Nothing is always good. If life was full of everything good and there was nothing bad, it would be synonymous to a child having an opportunity to eat candy all the time. Every thing works together for your good and the development of one's purpose.

It seems as if most of my worst experiences in life have become my greatest life teachers. My hardest tests have become some of the hardest life classes and I had to study and pray harder to pass those tests. Some assignments in life require a little more research and perseverance in order for me to pass and I have learned from the lessons what they were designed to teach me.

As strange as it may seem, some of my hardest tests in life were mounted in my life as posts to open some of the doors that I needed. There were opportunities that led me to the path God used in order to bring me to full circle. My business, Choice, Inc. eventually became a household name. It is known throughout the community just as it had been spoken of by my mom in a previous prophecy. The exposure that I gained at Choice afforded me access to world knowledge.

I continually tell my simple story. I have learned to recognize open doors and I have also learned to accept the doors that God has opted to close in my life. Furthermore, I have learned that God both opens and closes doors as He ordains lessons to be used for the good and His good pleasure. Ultimately, it is only my life story that has enlightened me to understand and accept my purpose and calling on this earth.

As I continually study the history of some of the world's greats they all have one thing in common and that's to acknowledge their own authentic trust is in God who vindicated the work he started in them with their birthright. When you use what was given to you by the Almighty your skills will become supernatural and will return supernatural results. The easiest and hardest part of doing what you were born to do is simple faith, surrender and obedience. Once you obtain those three traits, your dismal present will become your bright and promising future!

Back in the day, when I was living from paycheck to paycheck I still made sure that I invested in my own calling. If you expect someone else to believe in you, you must first believe in yourself and your own cause. I used my own money and made many sacrifices in order to ensure that I continued the work that I had started. I believed that when God wanted me to do something, He expected me to do it and allow him to supply all my needs according to his riches in glory. That's His business. My part is to take care of his business while he takes care of my business. It's like making an uneven exchange with God.

Eventually, my business experienced tremendous exponential growth. I mostly enjoyed the times when there were opportunities to work directly with hurting women. I often went out into the community and subscribed to events where I knew my target audience would be in attendance. I deliberately set up workshops at housing projects, churches, programs and other places where I could serve the hurting women that I had been assigned to serve. I even spent much time working with individuals one on one. When God opened doors I walked in and did the work that I was assigned to do.

I am driven and passionate about sharing myself and my skills with others! I love motivating people and I found that when I motivate others it also motivates me! Therefore, I specialize in mind-set change motivation. I love getting people pass the status quo.

There is always another way to view different situations. I like offering different perspectives on life while persuading individuals to develop their relevant skills through training. I found that most people only needed to sharpen their skill sets in order to become more marketable towards finding employment.

The process of developing and running my own business felt rather awkward at first. However, I had to work through my own learning curve. I was basically developing a process that would allow my clients to realize desired results. Initially a Choice office and class was set up at my local church where I purchased limited office space. I always desired to have my own place so I could implement my own curriculum and work without interference.

My experience was similar to Abraham's mandate where God told him to "Leave his country, his family, his friends and all his familiar surroundings and go to a place where he would show him." It seemed like that same type of calling was on my life.

I learned to keep my ears to the ground and to march to the beat of a different soldier. Although, I did receive lots of recognition and awards doing the work of Choice; my work was more about what God had assigned me to do. It was not about doing community work for money or recognition. I was using my birthright which was my God given talent to motivate, train and change lives. Doing business was a continuation of my testimony of "Faith" and what God could do with a little. Faith is only evidenced by the things you don't see.

As I was out there in the community operating my own business and touching the lives of the people who had been assigned to my account, people were attracted through my heartfelt desire to help them. Furthermore, I responded to the opened doors and God gave increase. Many people were helped and I was amazed!

My own personal testimony was that I preferred a job over welfare and training over hand outs. I wanted to become marketable, so, I took it upon myself to go back to school and develop the skills that I needed even in the mist of a dismal situation. Procrastination was not an option. I had to move right then and work hard even though my circumstances were prone to dictate something different. I wanted to help myself and work to help turn my own situation around. **God will bless you with a broom, but he expects you to use that broom and to sweep with it yourself. Marene, 101.**

Chapter 20

Following my Visions Lead

For years I had struggled with a husband so ill that he was unable to work. For years I shouldered the burden of providing for our five daughters. For years I stared into a future tethered to Public Assistance.

Ever tenacious, I endured repeated rough patches to earn a college degree. Next, I was rewarded with a job at Federal Express. I was indeed what you call a bona fide success story. Trouble was it wasn't success that I saw when I drove my neighborhoods streets. I saw too many women too much like myself year's ago-women wanting to work but too weary with the burden of raising children and too lacking in confidence to make tough, life-changing choices and stick to them. It hurts real badly when you're stereotyped.

Ultimately, I decided that succeeding alone wasn't enough. In 1996, I founded a non profit organization and named it, Choice, Inc. Using that non-profit community service organization, we set up a computer lab, and offered computer skills training, G.E.D. preparation, mind-set change motivational workshops, work ethic skills, professional imaging and job placement assistance. Also, through that program thousands of women (and men) were trained and found better lives for themselves and their families.

Although, we started by faith eventually we attracted funding from various sources. Often, it was a struggle and we didn't always have everything we needed to succeed. Therefore, we collaborated with many other city, state and federal social services. Eventually we had an opportunity to serve many hurting people at Choice, Inc. and we have multiple testimonies and successes to credit our work in the community. To date we have served close to ten thousand women and men, many of which are presently gainfully employed and successful. **"The harvest is truly plentiful but the laborers are few." KJV.**

It is very amazing what a person can do when she tries. A few years into our program I had an opportunity to do similar work in my hometown of Caruthersville, MO. I found that people are pretty much the same all over the world. Again, I went in and started from scratch in an attempt to offer the same services in Missouri as I had already been successful at doing in my own state.

Again, we collaborated with some of the establishments in that town and offered the same classes that were being offered in my state. Fortunately, we were allowed to utilize space at the Middle School and train more than 200 of that town's residents.

Eventually, our work attracted the Small Business Association which was located in Cape Girardeau MO. Some of our students subscribed to and were trained to start their own businesses. To date many of them have started businesses and some even have jobs as a result of the work we were able to do in that area.

If a project means anything to you, you won't mind using your own money, time or resources to develop it. I learned how to operate my business like any other business. I was already a professional. I already knew how to treat people. I had already learned management skills and I possessed an array of work and business experiences and expertise.

If God has a calling on your life he already has endowed you with the talents you'll need to fulfill your calling. The wise thing to do is to recognize what God has given you, accept what's genuinely yours and learn how to cultivate and develop it into what God can use in his big picture. You must also believe in yourself even when others refuse to believe in you. You must believe that you are going to achieve your many dreams regardless to how unrealistic they may seem. My philosophy is, **I can't allow obstacles to stop me because I can't get any where if I don't start somewhere. Marene, 101.**

It seemed like everything I touched turned into gold. When there were obstacles and stumbling blocks, I was guided around them and I was able to keep moving forward. I was focused, driven and excited which caught on and incited others around me. My work wasn't about reinventing the wheel, It was more about my one on one hands on methods of touching lives. I chose to become a friend to my clients and later I became their mentor.

I kept in mind the teachings that I had received from Kathleen Marx. She had already touched my life many years prior. I also kept in mind how much her coaching meant to me and how it had changed my life. Therefore, when I started my own non profit business I was also able to facilitate change in the lives of many others. I could not forget how grateful I felt after Kathleen Marx had helped to prep me for my future.

I wanted to pay her back in cash after my first management check. And her reply to me was, "Marene, every time you help someone else the way that I have helped you, you are paying me back for what I have invested in you." I will never forget those words. That statement also became a life lesson.

Many miracles followed me as I continued my work at Choice, Inc. because that work was ordained. For example, one Sunday evening my five daughters and I went out to eat at a Barnhill's restaurant. While chatting with an acquaintance at the steam table, we noticed that a waitress was standing there waiting to phase into our conversation. Both of us thought the other person knew her. However, it turned out that neither one of us actually knew her. It seemed like we all shared a commonality in our spiritually.

After the waitress merged her way into our conversation she started foretelling my acquaintance's future. Respectfully, I listened and observed. Then, she turned and looked at me and said, "God has given you something big to do and it is going to cause you to be known throughout the world." Of course this did sound good, but my mind could not soak it up at that time.

I had already planned to start Choice, Inc. at the time but, I had not yet executed my plan. Amazingly, I looked at her as she continued predicting. I was about to denounce her until she became somewhat personal and told me about my husband's illness and a few other personal things that were going on in my life that nobody else knew about. Who is this lady, I thought. At that point, she had my undivided attention. She went on and predicted that since I had chosen to obey Gods command to fulfill my calling in life that many new doors were going to open for me. She specifically described a very large door. She said that this door was so big that only a latch could close that door. She told me that I would also be world renowned. That gave me chills because I knew that she didn't know me and she didn't know anything about my dreams or vision. I was so moved by that prediction that I started crying.

When I returned to our table and my daughters noticed that I was crying, they thought that the lady had disrespected me. I assured them that we only had a spiritual conversation and that I was just moved by the conversation. They too witnessed seeing the young waitress who appeared to be around twenty two years of age. I told them that the waitress had prophesied to me about the future of my new business that I hadn't even started yet.

The next day out of sheer curiosity, I contacted the Barnhill's office at that same restaurant. I wanted another conversation with that waitress. Then, I was told by the manager that nobody her age or description worked there. I could not believe what I was hearing, so I insisted. Finally, I gave up. However, I couldn't dismiss the fact that I had spoken with that waitress. And, I certainly was not going to tell him about our conversation. I wanted to compliment her work in an attempt to possibly acquire another chance to converse with her.

After a second attempt to find the waitress to no avail, I contacted my acquaintance who also participated in a conversation with the waitress and witnessed the prophesying. To my surprise, she had also made an attempt to contact that same waitress. At that point, both of us recognized and acknowledged that we had encountered an angel. **"Be careful how you entertain strangers, you may be entertaining an angel unaware."**

A few days later my mama called me and she also prophesied that she had seen me in a vision traveling all over the world. She said that my business was going to become a household name just like coke. She told me that I would someday become a very successful business woman. She also told me that she saw my business being covered by various media outlets. She said, "Girl you are going to be in your local newspaper and many magazines."

Months after that, lots of good things started happening in my life and in my business development. I continued developing and establishing my business in the community. I was simply all over the place meeting people, taking classes and I was also started reaching out to train other women in the community.

During that time, while attending a month long grant writing class at United Way of the Mid-south; I learned through a conversation with a one of my student peers, that she was the wife of a writer for the Commercial Appeal. She asked me for permission to introduce me to her husband. She was very impressed with my business at Choice, Inc. A month later, he contacted me and interviewed me for an article. Later, my story was published in the local newspaper just like mama had previously prophesied.

A couple months later, I received a call from a freelance writer out of New Jersey who had read the article in the Commercial Appeal. She asked me if she could interview me and write another article on my story. Later, I learned that my story would be featured in a Premier Issue of a Magazine called Women & Success a Mary Kay product. When that magazine was published I rushed to Walgreens to purchase my copy. I can't tell you how I felt when I saw my picture in a national magazine. Again, that was exactly what my mama had prophesied to me!

As time progressed, I started receiving all kinds of calls from publishers requesting to publish my story. I was also contacted by Reader's Digest Magazine who later published an article. Next I received a call from African American Magazine, then the Metro Magazine, later, Grace Magazine, The Orange Mound Publisher, 50 Women that Make a Difference and FedEx Diversity magazine only, to name a few.

It seemed like everything that happened to me at that time, set off a chain reaction which continues until this day! I got calls from Radio and TV stations. I was applauded! Remember how my mama had prophesied about me being featured in the newspaper and other media outlets? That was my season and Choice was flourishing!

Doors were opening all over the place! I have had many good and bad experiences while operating in my calling and planting positive seeds in the community. We have experienced many successes even in the face of many adversities. We have had many successes, failures, connections, contributions, obstacles, donations and various doors of opportunities.

One time, my mama called me and told me that God told her to send me a contribution of twenty dollars ($20.00) and that I was to plant it as a seed in Choice, Inc's bank account. She specifically told me not to spend that $20.00 no matter how low my business account became. I obeyed her and planted the $20.00 seed in my Choice bank account and I would not touch it no matter what.

As time progressed, Choice, Inc.'s debt mounted and was getting out of control. Running that business started to become quite difficult! I had become accustomed to making ends meet and at that time, Choice was almost being operated out of my own pocket. Sometimes, all I had was my payroll check and my faith. At that time I was really struggling with that business.

I started falling behind in the bills. It seemed like I just didn't have enough money to make it and that I was going to lose the business. I prayed hard every day and continued to believe that I was on an assignment which was placed on me by God and that everything would work out. In the meantime, I was working overnight at Federal Express, taking care of my husband, my family. Additionally, I was running my Choice, Inc. business doing the day. It brought great pleasure to me as I watched those young ladies get their lives together and start succeeding just like I had already done.

There were times that I hardly knew how I was going to pay everything and everybody. At that time, I had acquired a building and of course I was responsible for the overhead whenever the business ran out of money. That situation was looking very bleak financially but I couldn't stop running the business. Too many people were being helped and I was getting gratification from doing my life's work. When I looked at the bills for Choice, Inc. they added up to over $7,000.00 and I was operating solely out of my pocket. I was digging deep without a cash flow. Nevertheless, I kept the faith and I knew that God would make provisions for the vision that he had given me. Consequently, I kept right on running Choice, Inc. as if the money was there.

During that time, preparations were being made for my daughter's wedding. Life was going on and we were living life. One Saturday evening after wedding shopping, we stopped by the post office to check the mail. Inside was a letter from the Women's Foundation containing a $20,000.00 contribution for Choice, Inc. I was stunned! Someone had made a $20,000.00 contribution to a little grassroots organization that I had so meticulously almost built with my own hands. That served to assure me that someone greater than I was investing in my vision. WHAT A MIRACLE!

Upon contacting the lady who had made that contribution, she told me to let her know if I needed anything else. She had seen me on a special that WMC-TV Channel 5 had featured on Choice, Inc. and she was impressed enough to plant a seed in the organization. I witnessed multiple miracles on a daily basis.

All our needs were met because of my obedience to the directions that were being whispered in my ear through my inner voice. My faith was real and I was fully surrendered to put my faith into action. Everything I did everyday was done solely by my faith in God and my work. Sometimes in my humanness I felt fear but I resorted to faith to get me out of reality so faith could work for me. I spent little time rationalizing because so many unusual things were happening on a daily basis. I was always amazed at how things turned out and how easy clientele was attracted to our work. When I couldn't see my way the universe was operating in unison with my vision.

It seemed like at those unpredictable times angels literally showed up and helped me through difficult situations. That was the Black Stallion horse that I was running behind in my dream. All of that work was rather surreal and spiritual. I was often led while soliciting board members, staff, volunteers, buildings, consultants, attorneys and accountants etc. Those resources were attracted to my work and they made enormous contributions. I learned to expect miracles on a daily basis. It seemed like I became very sad on days that there were no miracles. I was spoiled with faith! Life was becoming very exciting as I followed that horse. It was often stated that, "Choice is Marene and Marene is Choice."

I went to bed every night with a smile on my face knowing that I was tucked in my destined position in life and that my life was becoming an electrifying venture. Something was in my blood and it appeared that the "oil never ran out."

There were times when it seemed as if I was at my wit's end and I learned to pray and wait on my inner voice to tell me what to do next. Then I would step up believing that I was going in the right direction and things would always work out. Things that we needed as we continued to operate Choice would simply show up in time to get expected results.

The work was not easy but by faith it was achievable. I was happy as I did the work of Choice and it took my mind off the negative things that were going on in my life like my husband's illness. God kept me centered and gave me the strength to deal with family life, working, running my business and finding some type of stability in my own life. Faith in what I believed in was almost all I had going for me at that time.

One day, while driving past a dilapidated housing project in the city, something went out of my spirit and my interest was drawn to that area. Suddenly, I felt a desire to meet the women there because I felt that would be a great place to offer Choice, Inc.'s services. Later, I was approved to facilitate Choice, Inc.'s training at that housing project and again many hurting women were trained, helped and empowered.

I expressed to them how much I believed that if they tried, they too could become successful and have better lives. They had a purpose for being and I was willing to help them to identify and find themselves. I told them how I personally had left the welfare rolls and went back to school and worked hard educating myself and how I had beaten the odds. I identified with people who reminded me of my past life and my exodus through my own self development. Sometimes I had to work single handedly and many times I worked without pay most of the time. I was happy to give back to the community that had given so much to me. Of course, it took money to make manuals and curriculum and to buy computers and other needed items and if I needed them it seemed like I was always able to obtain them one way or the other. Doing that work was like an art and I was constantly painting a new picture!

Work at Choice, Inc. always made me feel exhilarated! It seemed like I got another wind and a new energy when I was operating fully in my calling. My desire was to touch the lives of other hurting women even as I was hurting myself. I could identify with their pain because I had experienced much pain myself. Remember my role in my dream about the "Field of Pain?" I was trying to help as many people as I could through Choice, Inc. That's how I was able to find all those hurting women in life who were crying out for help.

I had experienced pain and rejection before while seeking a job without the proper skills. I simply went back to school to sharpen my skills and afterwards I was qualified to seek employment. I applied myself, achieved the necessary skills and training and reached my goals. Then, at Choice I was able to design the necessary specific training that boosted the skill-sets of others. That was my "Marene Potion." If it worked for me it could also work for others.

As I developed my business with the help of God and with the many people who helped me along the way, I learned how my uniqueness and creativity had carved out a niche' for me to reach my goals. I wanted to see others also learn how to find appropriate resources and create new lives for themselves and their children just like I had done in my own life. That was the ultimate in "Celebrating my life's lessons!"

One of the most mysterious things about a God given talent is its uniqueness. Your talent is an insert that comes packaged inside you at birth. At some point in life you must plug in to that talent in order for it to work the way it is designed to work. Your talent is a natural part of who you are. It is not hard to refine and use it. For example, when a person can sing, it doesn't take lots of effort for him to sing. That person has a beautiful voice that only needs a little cultivating. That voice will be illustrious and can not be duplicated. **When people hear someone who has a talent to sing, they learn to identify that person by their voice. That voice actually is distinguished and it authenticates that person. Marene, 101.**

My uniqueness has been established by the God of the Universe. I know exactly what I am supposed to do in my life and I am doing it. My life's lessons and experiences have gleamed pearls of riches out of my life and eliminated excuses that can hinder my success. When I share my own life's accomplishments people can also witness that all things are possible.

I seriously believe that when a person is working in his calling there is a power working in unison with him. Your expectations are limitless and effective. You can intellectually pick up on waves from the universe like radio signals. Your higher energy will attract signals to your field that will deliver you to the doorsteps of your calling and purpose. Therefore, you cannot allow the negative forces of doubt and fear to penetrate and overthrow your efforts.

Chapter 21

The Attraction of Faith

I once attracted a well known TV personality to come to Memphis and speak at a fundraiser for our organization. That was another one of my faith moves. I moved forward planning that event as if we already had everything that we needed to have the event.

After a meeting at the Adams Mark Hotel I learned that I needed to make a $500.00 deposit to retain event space at the hotel. I only had three days to pay the deposit and I had no way to obtain the money. Within a few couple days I received a card from a couple who were celebrating their 3rd wedding anniversary. They both mutually agreed to make a $500.00 dollar contribution to Choice, Inc. signifying a wedding gift to each other. That turned out to be the exact amount of the deposit I needed. Was that another miracle?

Again, while we were experiencing sluggish ticket sales one of my neighbors recommended that I contact a local radio station which turned out to be a God send! I gained an interview at the station that rendered sold out tables for the event including multiple media coverage and a standing only crowd. The moral of this story is faith worked again and the whole universe worked in unison with the vision.

It seemed like everything that I thought about and moved on brought miracles. I marvel over the fact that Choice took on a life of its own.

There were plenty ups and downs but we were vigilant in our work. Most importantly thousands of people managed to receive training and change their lives and mind sets. That work was about alleviating the pain that I had discovered in that open "Field of Pain" that I dreamed about. Many people helped me to impel my business along.

One time a loyal board member introduced me to a very wealthy woman who I reached out to hug when I first saw her. She was impressed with my hug. You never know how the anointing is working and the things that endear people to you. She asked me to promise to remain exactly the way I am. You never know what the drawing card is that attracts people to your work. Although her statement sounded rather strange, I agreed. In her warm spirited way she asked me to meet her at the Housing Authority. Later she was instrumental in connecting me with an opportunity to do contract work with the Housing Authority. She commented on her respect for the work that I was doing in the community.

Such accolades as the above demonstrate how taking steps that are directed towards your calling render unlimited opportunities. Faith requires one to make a move without seeing any evidence of how the results will play out. **You do the work first, then, you will see the results after you start the work. Faith must have wheels of action in order to move and work on. Marene, 101.**

I never applied for awards they were attracted to my work. I was always amazed at how the energy that came with my obedient spirit tapped into the universal energy that attracted positive waves and gave rise to our work. We remained busy and focused as we delightfully worked in the community. It felt like we were cooking something good and people were coming to eat our food. That was also establishing our credibility and would later prove to make it possible for us to continue our work.

The most important thing is that many women were being touched and were becoming empowered on how to navigate through their own lives, changing their mind-sets while enhancing their skill sets towards self actualization. They could then testify that they had a different outlook on life. We started hearing comments like, "I never thought that I could make this happen in my life but Ms Austin at Choice, Inc. inspired me to try."

I enjoyed beating the pavement; networking, learning new strategies, receiving mentoring by some of the best in the field, taking classes, getting trained, teleconferencing, communicating and collaborating and developing my own programs that were personally carved out with my own hands. I was also intrigued when soliciting new board of directors and their cooperation with the organization.

There were many ups and downs, joys and struggles and accomplishments from day to day, as well as from year to year. My faith was triggered when I was listening to my inner voice and following its guide. I believed that developing Choice, Inc. was one of my birthrights and it brought me great joy to work at it. It was like a natural function for me and something that was plugged in me at birth. It didn't matter that it required that I remain outside the box or that I defy tradition. It was working and that was all that mattered. I experienced all types of obstacles but with the help of God, my inner voice, strangers/angels and many interesting parties we continue our work at Choice. We ran our business through the sunshine, through the rain, through the storms, and through various changes in community's interests.

I worked when people believed in me and I worked when people did not believe in me. I also worked a full time job while running Choice, Inc. I faced many surmountable challenges, such as, remaining a caretaker for my husband, being a mother, a wife and a housekeeper etc. **Life doesn't offer you a sabbatical in order to fulfill your calling. Life gives you experiences and you learn the lessons needed to fulfill your purpose. Marene, 101. There aren't breaks and shortcuts to use your faith. You step out into the dark and follow your dream, along with whatever else you're doing. Marene, 101.** I was very committed to doing the work. That is the kind of drive and energy that goes along with your calling and it is phenomenal!

I loved the feeling of swimming in the pool of my vision. The calling that was on my life was as real as my life was real. I'd rather do my life's work than to eat, sleep or drink. I found the time to do something at Choice, Inc. everyday no matter what. We were certainly climbing our ladder to our destination. All of this has happened to a little lady who set out to obey the calling that was on her life.

I started out as a little broken vessel and my brokenness started healing with doing my life's work. Yes, I was a former welfare recipient using my own life's lessons and experiences and seeking to rebuild the life of someone else that had buried dreams and were in too much pain to go forward. All this had happened to me after I had come to the end of my own "broken pot" that appeared to be unrecoverable. I had learned by then that, **"Nobody can call cursed, what God himself has called "blessed." It is not up to others what you do with the Scroll (gift) that God had placed in your hand. Marene, 101.**

As my life and my business progressed my growth reached another level of testing. There were times when my work was tested in order to build resilience and to prepare me for the next level. I have faced many chilly winds of adversity in my life and in my work. After working for years in business and working through many challenges and complexities we came to a turn in the road that would lead us in another direction.

Sometimes I felt fear and it was somewhat scary when I stepped outside my spiritual mind-set and looked at situations through my natural eyes. Nevertheless, in my spiritual mind I knew that the Black Stallion had taken off again and that I was running very fast in a different direction. There I was again, jumping ditches and running through water and again "Running with the Vision." All I could do was hold on to the scroll that was placed in my hand and "Run with the Vision." I had to do what the horse did and I continued running.

Looking back and going forward, I learned that some things are for a reason and many opportunities are only for a season. I also learned how to determine when a season had ended and how it had prepared me to enter into my next season. You can not take the summer into the fall and the winter has a life of it own. When the winter of life comes, you must take off the swimming suit and put on a coat. You must be willing to change when the seasons change. The universe is constantly turning pages and you must realize that you are being led by a higher power than yourself. There will always be new ventures out on the horizon. Consequently, I had to keep my eyes on the Black Stallion and keep up with that horse if I planned on maintaining my calling.

Within a few more years I was fortunate to connect with two of my former classmates, Ron & Rich. After careful planning we collaborated and created an avenue to do some serious work in our former hometown of Caruthersville Missouri. That all started as a follow up and mutual concern that all of us shared after the town experienced one of their most horrific tornados. Our work was most interesting and challenging and we continued to grow in our efforts. The Black Stallion started driving me again as I noticed that there could be an opportunity for us to bring Choice, Inc.'s work to that town and touch lives.

We later expanded the work of Choice, Inc. into the Missouri area and implemented entrepreneur development and training. After the success of that project we continued our training in the area for the next three years before my inner voice spoke and told me that my assignment was completed. Subsequently, more than two hundred individuals were served during that training period. Some individuals chose to drive to Memphis for Choice training and consequently, others participated in a weekend Choice retreat in Memphis as we navigated through our assignment.

After working in Caruthersville, MO and sustaining many challenges, Lincoln University in Jefferson City, MO eventually contacted me and worked out a plan for us to use their facility, The Lincoln Extension Building. Later, Lincoln University through their Land Grant Program, also eventually contracted with Choice, Inc. and together we served people in the Caruthersville Community.

Chapter 22

A Few Choice Stories in Caruthersville

One Saturday morning I while driving to Caruthersville I realized that I hardly had enough gas money to make the round trip that day but I had to keep my commitment to my students in Caruthersville. I stopped in Arkansas to get some gas. I gave the attendant my last twenty dollar bill and hurriedly, I forgot to pump the darn gas. I panicked when I noticed thirty miles out that my empty light was blinking. Needless to say, I drove back to the service station and was denied a refund. The attendant told me that the sale was closed and that they could not refund my money. After speaking to the manager to no avail, I accepted the fact that the station was not going to be fair with me. I needed a miracle to get to Caruthersville.

Reluctantly, I gave up, left the station with a determination that I was going to make it to Caruthersville that day and nothing and nobody was going hinder me. I had to fall back on my faith again and believe it could be done. I stopped at another station down the road and raked up another seven dollars from the bottom of my purse. I had about seventy nine (79) miles to travel on $7.00 worth gas. Lord did I need a miracle that day! After calling and informing one of my faithful students, Viola, of my dilemma, she told me that she would meet me in Blytheville, AR. if I could make it that far. Let's pray and believe was my reply because I was on my way. Needless to say, I believed and I did make it to Blytheville on the $7.00 worth gas which didn't even change the status of the empty light. When I made it to Blytheville, my student Viola filled up my gas tank with her credit card. That was another miracle and another angel experience.

When I arrived at the Lincoln Extension Building that day, I witnessed one of the largest crowds ever! Lots of new students joined our class. When I walked in, Pat was running the program and holding the audience in place. Helena and Catherine were serving a nice continental breakfast and nobody even had a clue that I'd had such a challenging experience prior to my arrival. After that day, Choice, Inc.'s student base continued to grow and expand. A larger radius area in the Bootheel gradually enrolled in our program. I continued driving the two hundred mile round trip to Caruthersville because the pulse beat was high for the Choice training and I was very excited as I operated in my element!

I encountered many miracles while working in the Missouri area. One great example was; one day while a small of my supporters were meeting with me mat Apple Barrel in Hayti, MO, we noticed a gentleman who was pacing back and forth pass our table. Finally, he stopped and asked if we were women of God or something. I told him that we were just working in the community trying to help people. Then he got emotional and emptied his pockets of all the money that he had on our table. He wanted to make a contribution to someone who was doing God's work. He also confessed that his work did not allow him to serve God correctly. The man donated $40.00 to our work and I needed gas money to get back to Memphis. That was another miracle.

Another time when I was traveling to Missouri one of my tires blew out. I stopped and looked under the hood because I had no idea where that loud noise was coming from. The funny thing was that all my tires were still standing. I continued to drive my car slowly towards my destination, while it was rocking and making loud noises. Finally, a nice young man came by and stopped to help me. He checked the car and found the big plug in the tire. He couldn't understand why the tire was not flat, not to mention that I did not have a spare tire. He committed to trailing me to my destination to make sure I arrived safely. The young man followed slowly behind me all the way to the Lincoln Extension Building in Caruthersville, MO. Was that another miracle and another angel?

Sometimes I think that God is having fun when he allows things like that to happen. Experiences like that show us who God really is. After class that day one of my students took her spare tire off her husband's truck and donated it to me. That's what I call, "People Helping People."

Once I completed that assignment in Missouri again more than thirty individuals had completed the entrepreneurship training and to date some of them have started a business, enhanced their existing business or are aspiring to become business owners. My work proved to be meaningful in the Missouri area. And, I gained many new friends and associates in that area. Our work coincided right along with the work that I was already doing in Memphis.

One day my inner voice spoke to me and said something like this: "doing business in deep waters" and for some reason, I felt that I would find the answer to that statement in the bible. Later I found a Bible scripture, **Psalms 119:23** and it goes like this: **KJV**

"Those who go down to the sea in ships, who do business on great waters, they see the works of the Lord, and his wonders in the deep. For he commands and raises the stormy wind; which lifts up the waves of the sea. They mount up to the heavens, they go down again to the depths; their souls melt because of trouble. They reel to and fro, and stagger like a drunken man, and are at their wit's end. Then they cry out to the Lord in their trouble. And, he brings them out of their distresses. He calms the storm, so that its waves are still. Then they are glad because they are quiet; then he guides them to their desired haven (end).

That scripture remained in the back of my mind as I faced many adversities, obstacles such as: jealousy, despair, and rejection. Things were not always pleasant for me, but I remain focused on my Black Stallion and continue to run hard behind that horse. I had that Scroll in my hand as I had to continue "Running with the Vision."

Those deep waters signified oceans. That represented vast "Chilly Winds of Adversity." That adversity eventually entered in my business life. There were lies told which affected the very foundation of my business. The truth is the light but lies are dark and confusing. For a long time I didn't understand what was going on so I just stood still, kept my mouth closed and prayed for strength. I also knew that just as the above scripture stated that at the end I would reach my desired haven. God always goes along with you through every dark tunnel that's set before you. He protects his work that he has started in you and you can be assured that he will stand by you through thick and thin. Sometimes family, friends and associates will leave you but if they go there is a purpose for it. I needed that experience to get me to where I am today and to keep me focused on my real friend who is the God of the universe.

Adversity in a business is a necessary malevolence. Since I started my first business I have had to catch multiple curve balls and direct them back and keep on pressing. Instead of trying to figure out the reasons why, I catch the balls and run fast towards second base in an attempt to win the game because the victory has already been won for me.

One of my greatest lessons has been to learn the proper way to handle adversity. Your response can make you or it can break you. Therefore, adversity is to be treated like a storm. The first thing to remember is that it is a storm and storms don't last always. You respond to a storm by retreating for cover. You respect the dynamics of that storm and wait until the high winds settle down before you exit. Then you emerge with caution. It's your responsibility to protect yourself from the weather. I have learned how to remain peaceful and stay in a position of survival so at the end of a storm I can grow from the experience. Nothing happens without a reason, especially when you are on a mission and fulfilling your assignment in life.

All the things that have happened to me were all about my vision. It has been all about the work. Now it's all about the, "C E L E B R A T I O N!" I went where the vision went. I jumped the ditches in life, I ran through the waters of life, then I slowed my pace as the vision slowed its pace and I trotted, as the vision trotted. **As life teaches lessons one must recognize when he is involved in a life's lessons and identify the purpose of the experience. The day will surely come when he can celebrate his life's Lessons. Marene, 101.**

When the time came for me to write this book, I felt an urge to just get started. Again, without the appropriate expertise I started writing. I just stepped out there again in the dark and followed the directions of the voice inside my spirit. I venture to ascertain that everyone has a conscience that speaks to them all the time. It all happens somewhat similar to the story of the "Field of Dreams," which states; "Build it and they will come."

People who sit around and make plans and wait for the plans to develop into the work usually fail in their efforts. It doesn't work that way. Your work will be carved out as you decide to follow in blind obedience. You must remain faithful to your work and you must also put that faith into action in order for the plan to come together.

Now, I have come to a point in my career where I can,

"CELEBRATE LIFE'S LESSONS!"

THE BEGINNING!

THANKS FOR YOUR GENEROUS CONTRIBUTIONS!

TRACI ABRAM

CHARITY AUSTIN-HICKS

CURZETTA AUSTIN

JOE & PATRICIA CAGLE

BOBBY COLEMAN

VIOLA COLEMAN

SHIRLEY HARRIS

DONLI HAYES

RITA HAYES

DAN JONES SR.

LARRY JONES SR.

RENEE & NATHANIEL JONES

ODESSIA JONES

LAVITA LEWIS

BONNIE & JOHN LEWIS

DANA LYNN

MARJORIE MOORE

ADRIENNE NELSON

RONALD NELSON

RON PAYNE

QUEEN PITTS

YOUR CONTRIBUTIONS HAVE MADE
MY BOOK PROJECT A SUCCESS!!

I especially thank my editors, Mrs. Jeanna Brandon and Ms Curzetta Monik' Austin for your patience with me. Also a special thanks to Adrienne Nelson who designed the cover of my book. I could never have completed this book without your help.

Thanks, Marene J. Austin

About the Author Marene J. Austin

Marene J. Austin, Author, Celebrate Life's Lessons, Business Owner-C.E.O. MA, Enterprises, Jewelry Artist, Founder/ Executive Director, Choice, Inc. since 1996, Former Instructor, Professional Development, Anthem College approximately, Retired Operations Manager, Federal Express Corporation (Hub Ops) Former Contractor, Department of Human Services, United Way of the Mid-South, Friends for Life, Memphis Housing Authority, Lincoln University Land Grant Program, Jefferson City Missouri, Former Lab Supervisor, Shelby State Community College.

Author/Self Publisher, Jewelry Artist, Motivational Speaker, Entrepreneur Development, Coach, Leader, Consultant, Business Owner, Curriculum & Program Designer and Community Advocate.

One of Marene's greatest achievements has been to become an Author and to take advantage of the opportunity to Self-Publish her own first book.

Now Marene proudly presents her first book entitled, "CELEBRATE LIFE'S LESSONS." She takes great pride in acknowledging that all the thoughts in her book are original. All the stories in this book are true and factual. Marene's, 101 quotes are her very own original work. Her goal is to find and seize every opportunity to touch lives through her gift to motivate and inspire others and to offer some healing methods that can alleviate some of the pain that exists in the universe.

We hope you enjoyed this book. If you would like to receive free Motivation and Inspiration or additional information please contact:

MA Enterprises via misschoice2@hotmail.com

Or web address http://www.celebratelifelessons.com

You may also follow us on Facebook, Twitter, Thumbtack, Google, Myspace, & Linkedin. Personal Contact# 901-382-7806

You may also sign up at http://celebratelifelessons.com and subscribe to receive daily motivational & inspirational emails. You also may be eligible to win various prizes & rewards. We welcome opportunities for Interviews/Appearances/Speaking Engagements/Book Signings.

At your request you may receive event Announcements, Discounts & Offers, Special Events, Product Highlights, Free Excerpts, Giveaways and much more . . .

http://www.celebratelifelessons.com